'For a traveller, a household kitchen in a strange land is usually a remote destination, but it is one that tells the "truth" about food and everyday life,' says Nao Saito, architect and designer from Japan. A kitchen is usually thought of as a particular arrangement of space. But a space is not just a fixed physical structure – it is also fluid, shaped by the way in which people use it.

Keeping this connection in mind, Nao Saito set out to explore a colourful variety of kitchens during her stay in South India. With her abiding interest in people and cookery, she finally came up with this richly perceptive travelogue, bringing together floor plans, sketches, photographs, impressions, recipes and conversation.

In the process, South Indian kitchens emerge as more than just domestic spaces: they are distinctive ways of living and relating to the world.

TRAVELS
THROUGH
SOUTH INDIAN
KITCHENS

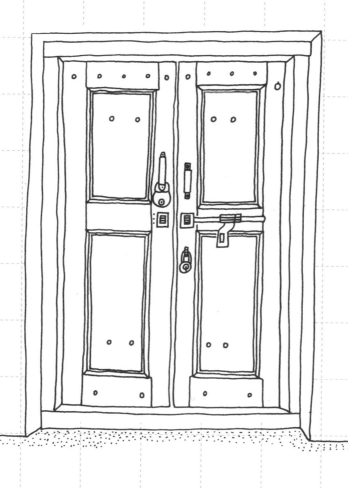

Nao Saito

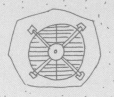

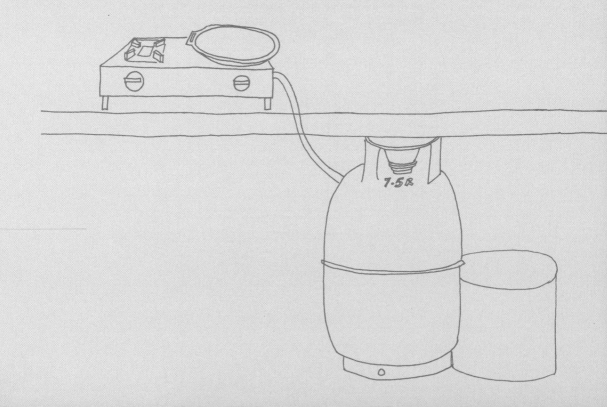

CONTENTS

WHY SOUTH INDIAN KITCHENS?

I am a Japanese woman from Tokyo, and an architect by profession. I like designing on a small scale, particularly furniture or interiors. I've also worked with museum educators and other architects to re-imagine museum spaces with educational programmes, and to come up with plans for new buildings. This is why I'm drawn to the space of each kitchen I describe in this book; the description explores the way in which a particular space influences what we do – at the same time, it is created by how people use it.

In all my work, if there is one form that has inspired my thinking, it would be the picture book. For instance, you could think of a sofa as an object on which two people can sit and read a story together, while reflecting on where they are.

I've had the opportunity to spend time in Finland, where I studied design. While I was there, I discovered how people engage – in the course of their everyday lives – with a strong and beautiful natural world. It was this kind of connection – of a people to their environment and culture – which drew me to India. Of course, the Indian context is very different from the Finnish one – it is culturally quite distinct.

I'd never imagined that I would actually travel to India, so when the opportunity came up, I was excited, but nervous. It happened like this: G., the publisher of Tara Books, had been invited to Japan to conduct a workshop on the form of the book, for illustrators and designers. I was one of the participants, and the two of us got on well together. Before leaving, G. invited me for a residency at their publishing house in Chennai, South India. Things moved quickly after that, and a few months later, I actually arrived in Chennai.

This book is the result of that three month stay. In these pages, I've tried to capture the air I breathed during that time, but through a particular lens: the kitchen. The idea to focus my experience around kitchens arose serendipitously, when I walked into the cooking area of my apartment in Chennai. It was familiar, but also quite strange. I've always been interested in food and kitchen tools, and this, combined with my interest in architecture and people, gave rise to the idea behind this project: I wanted to travel through a place not by exploring its public spaces, but through the heart of people's homes – their kitchens. I wanted to focus not only on architecture, but also capture a lived sense of space, cooking, people and conversation. For a traveller, a household kitchen in an alien land is a remote place, something she rarely encounters. Yet each of us has a kitchen at home, and we associate it with distinctive scents, tastes, conversation, laughter, and perhaps also solitude. And this makes it possible for us to actually reach out and try to understand what is going on in a kitchen in a faraway land.

But I'm getting ahead of myself here. Many of these insights came to me only during the course of my visits, and after I had spent some time reflecting on what I had experienced. The way the project unfolded was actually quite simple and spontaneous: I proposed my idea to G. and the others at the publishing house, and they were very enthusiastic. We decided to structure it around visits to people's homes – and to begin with, our own colleagues in the publishing house, who all came from very different communities and backgrounds. The visits gradually widened to include friends, and friends of friends.

The idea was not just to view kitchens, but to spend time with cooks as they created meals – and be invited to share food and conversation. The whole thing was not minutely planned – the visits were mostly informal, and sometimes led spontaneously to other encounters. I love meeting people, and this made it easy for me, as did the generous hospitality and openness that is so typical of India. I made many lasting friendships as a result, and still remember with gratitude all the wonderful people who invited me into their kitchens, and cooked for me and their loved ones. I've also tried out many of the dishes they cooked, here in my Tokyo kitchen – and discovered that cooking a foreign recipe in my own surroundings is a powerful way of linking those South Indian kitchens to mine.

Usually, when I travel, my tools are my camera, sketch book, and pencil: this has stayed the same during this journey. But there's one difference: while I write and sketch a lot during the usual course of my work or travels, it's just for myself, and not meant for others. So with this piece of work, I feel a certain sense of responsibility, something I owe to people who treated me so well, and welcomed me so warmly into their homes. They deserve my complete honesty... so I resisted the temptation of hiding moments of ignorance or anxiety, which did come up now and then.

I'd like to leave them with this image: there is a rice field, in the south of Tokyo, nestling in a small valley. For some reason, there are banana trees growing there, even though bananas are not part of the Japanese landscape. On weekends, I help out in this field. And as I walk by those trees, I sometimes smell the scent of banana flowers – and am transported to my beloved Chennai.

I remember that guests are served food on a banana leaf.

A KITCHEN WITH NO IDEA

I arrive at my guest house in Chennai, South India, where I am to stay for three months, working as a designer in a publishing house. My apartment is a small red attic-like space. I see the small kitchen, in the middle. If I stand at the counter, I can reach in all directions – I can actually touch the stove, the sink and the refrigerator. My first impressions tell me that it is a functional kitchen. There are several jars with spices and lentils (called *dal* in Hindi and *parruppu* in Tamil) on the shelf. There is also a hanging rack suspended from the ceiling, filled with things. I like it all at first sight.

But at the same time, I don't know what to do. I turn the gas on, but the stove doesn't light up. (Much later, I would practise many times with the gas lighter to get the stove going, but I could never do it very well). Now I notice the gas cylinder under the counter. I've seen such cylinders only outside homes. I look at the shelf: so many jars of beans! Will I ever learn which bean goes into the making of which dish? I see a water can on top of the fridge. Is that water I can drink? But hold on, am I okay drinking water out of a can? Then I discover tiny – unfamiliar – pans in the shelf under the counter. There's also

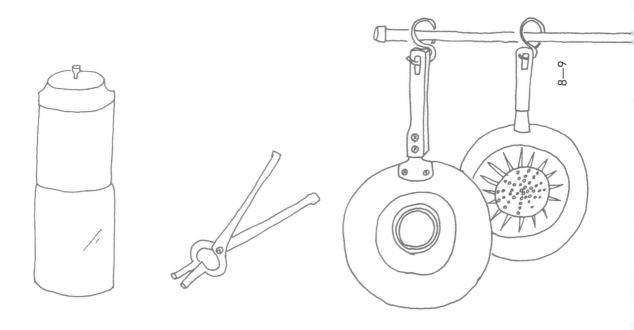

a vessel that looks like a stacked stainless steel tower, like
a futuristic building. Why is everything here made of stainless steel?

A Kitchen with No Idea. The thought pops into my mind that first day
in Chennai, standing in the middle of that kitchen. I'm shocked. I love
cooking and whenever I travel to foreign countries, I find some nice
ingredients and very quickly make something with them. This is one
of the few skills that I possess… until this moment, at least. Now my
first encounter with a South Indian kitchen leaves me with a very
strange feeling, a kind of excitement mixed with anxiety.

It also gives rise to the germ of an idea: it is from this kitchen
that I set off, to explore and discover other South Indian kitchens.
Once the idea is in place, the project is not hard to follow through.
I discover that my colleagues at the publishing house are a very
mixed group, and over the next few months, I will be welcomed
not only into their kitchens, but also to those of their friends.

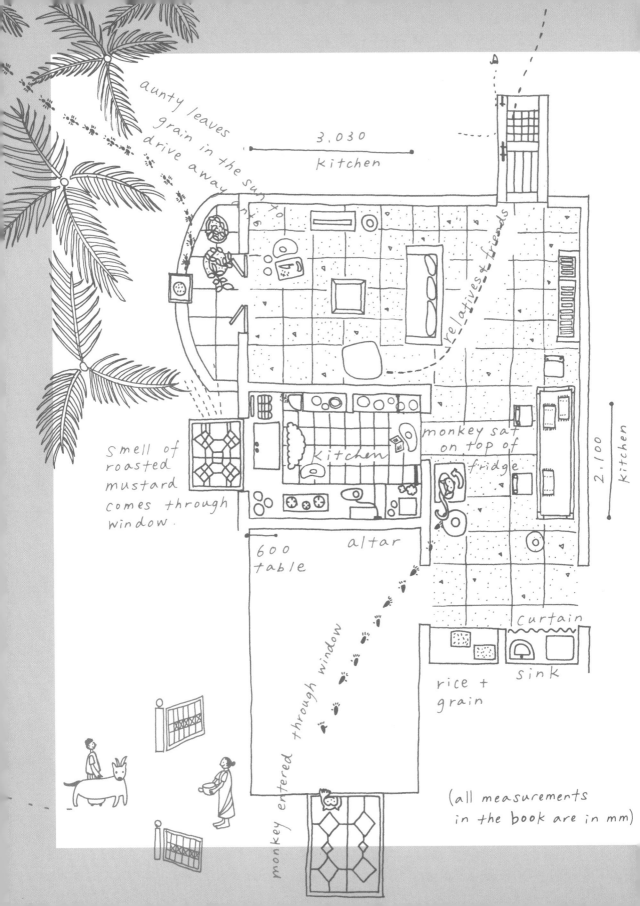

aunty leaves grain in the sun to dry drive away ants

3.030
kitchen

relatives & friends

monkey sat on top of fridge

smell of roasted mustard comes through window.

kitchen

2.100
kitchen

altar

600
table

Curtain

sink

rice + grain

monkey entered through window

(all measurements in the book are in mm)

EXPANDING KITCHEN

10.00 AM. I AM AT AUNTY S.' DOOR. She is my colleague G.'s mother. Aunty S. welcomes me, wearing a light green starched cotton sari. The entrance leads into the living room which opens out into a small balcony, framed by French windows. They are open and let in the bright morning sun. There is lots of morning light everywhere in the apartment. It is located in the inner city, close to one of Chennai's older neighbourhoods. Aunty S. lives with her daughter, G. The other member of the household is P., a young woman studying to be a surgeon. She is G.'s friend's daughter.

Lunch will be at 1.00 pm today, I hear, since G. plans to leave home for work only in the afternoon. Aunty S. starts preparing to cook. She says that the first thing she does in the morning is to pray at an altar that is located at the entrance of her kitchen. There are many Hindu gods in that altar. There is also a picture of her husband who has passed away.

The first thing to do, she tells me, is to cut vegetables. 'On days that G. goes to work, I start cutting vegetables at 7.00 in the morning. Otherwise at 8.00.'

Aunty S. goes into the kitchen, in her beautiful sari, without putting on an apron. When she returns to the living room from the kitchen, I see how it is connected to other spaces in the house. Aunty S. is carrying a bowl with vegetables, a knife and a cutting board. She lowers herself on to the floor. 'Using a knife is a new thing for me' she says, beginning to slice green beans. 'I was always used to an *arivalmannai*, our traditional cutting and grating tool.'

I look out and see a stainless steel bowl sunning on the balcony ledge. 'That's grain,' says Aunty S., following my gaze. 'Ants got into the grain, so I put it out in the sun. They'll leave, because it gets too hot for them

egg-plants are
tender

'I feel
comfortable'

sliced
egg-plants
in water

aunty sits on floor
to cut vegetables.

there.' If I were her, I would throw the whole thing away. But here she is, sunbathing the ants, and that too with a kind a word for them!

After she's finished cutting the vegetables, Aunty S. goes into the kitchen and turns on the stove. She has an efficient way of cooking: she piles rice, *dal* and vegetables into small vessels and puts them into a pressure cooker. When that's done, she puts a small frying pan on the second burner of the stove and lights it. She pours a bit of oil into the pan, and then throws in some mustard seeds. A lovely smell of popped mustard wafts out of the pan. 'When we have guests,' says Aunty S., 'They wait for dinner, in the living room or the balcony, chatting. When they smell the mustard they know dinner is ready.'

Aunty S. takes an hour and a half to cook. Lunch is ready at one and we sit down to eat as scheduled. Today we are eating *kootu*, a stew made of eggplant and dal, and *rasam*, a tamarind broth. There is also green beans with coconut, rice, cracked wheat and yogurt.

Aunty S. talks to me as we all eat. 'One day, when G. and I were eating like we are now, we heard a sound, a thud. When we looked up, we saw this big monkey sitting on top of the refrigerator! There are dense trees in our neighbourhood and lots of monkeys living in them. They come into apartments when they can't find enough food. The monkey that morning came in through the window in G.'s room.'

I'm startled by the story, and look up from the table at the fridge several times. In contrast to my nervousness, Aunty S. is relaxed and continues to eat. I ask her where she gets her milk, because I haven't yet figured out where to buy it. 'Nowadays, it is delivered home, but,' adds Aunty S. 'Ten or fifteen years ago, a milkman with his cow would come to our house – our old house – and milk her in front of the entrance. We'd bring a vessel and he'd fill it up!'

'smell of fried mustard
means dinner is ready'

After lunch, Aunty S. picks up a tool from the shelf. It's the arivalmannai she mentioned earlier, traditionally used to cut vegetables sitting on the floor. 'I can't find people to sharpen the cutting blade anymore, so I don't use it. But I keep it because sometimes my relatives visit, and help with cooking. They need this. Back then, on special occasions, women would gather to cook. They'd sit together on the floor and cut vegetables.'

Women continue to come to this house – many of G.'s friends do. The morning I was there I noticed that all the windows and doors were open, and that impression of openness says a lot about Aunty S.'s attitude towards others.

Later, when I tell G. how flexibly Aunty S. uses space while she cooks, she says, 'In her head, she still cooks in the big kitchen in our old house. That was a huge space.' Next time around, I will ask Aunty S. about her last kitchen, of which she doesn't have any photos anymore.

This is how I begin my travels through South Indian kitchens. Aunty S.'s place is the first, and here, to my surprise, I realise that the kitchen need not be a single room. It can expand to other spaces inside and even outside. The working surface flows from the table to the floor, expanding from the kitchen to the living room and the balcony. The space seems to expand beyond what I could have imagined. It's a place where not just people but all kinds of living creatures come and go. Aunty S.'s relatives, and now G.'s friends, the lady who does domestic work for her, the monkey, the ants, a cow... all invited and uninvited creatures.

SAMBAR

RASAM

you can put hot pot directly on the table

more
red chilli

more
black pepper

table top : granite

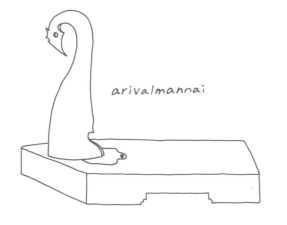

arivalmannai

`CLOCK is important for pressure cooker.`

`BLOW before use to check if air goes in.` sometimes there may be ants inside!

put weight

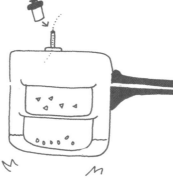

piling up ingredients very effective

1. low flame

2. high flame

3. no flame for 15 min.

Aunty S.'s Kathirikai Kootu
Stew with Eggplant and Dal

Serves 4

8 small eggplants
a small cup of chickpeas
a marble sized piece of tamarind
a pinch of turmeric powder
salt to taste
a pinch of asafoetida powder

Spice Mixture

2 tbsp. oil
2 dried red chillies
2 tbsp. whole coriander seeds
1 tbsp. urad dal
2 tbsp. grated coconut
1 tbsp. mustard seed
a few curry leaves

Soak the tamarind in water for around half an hour, then squeeze out the pulp. Wash and cover the chickpeas with water, then cook it until they soften. A pressure cooker is helpful. Cut the eggplants into cubes and soak them in water – this will prevent them from oxidising. Boil the eggplant cubes in the tamarind water. Meanwhile, prepare the spice mixture. Heat 1 tbsp. of oil in a small pan, and fry the coriander seeds, red chillies, and *urad dal* until it turns golden. Add the coconut and turn off the flame. Grind together in an electric blender. Pour this paste into the tamarind and eggplant mixture, add the cooked chickpeas and bring the kootu to a short boil. Heat l tbsp. oil in a small frying pan, add asafoetida, curry leaves and mustard seeds until they pop. Pour this tempering over the stew.

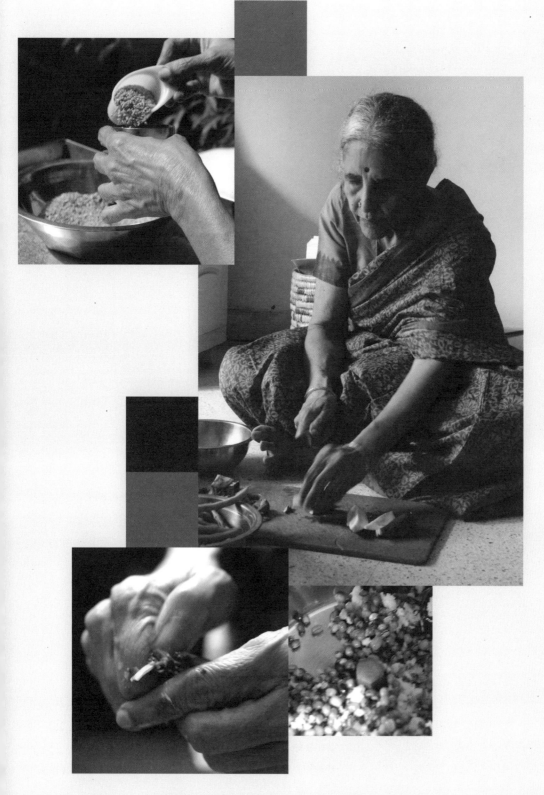

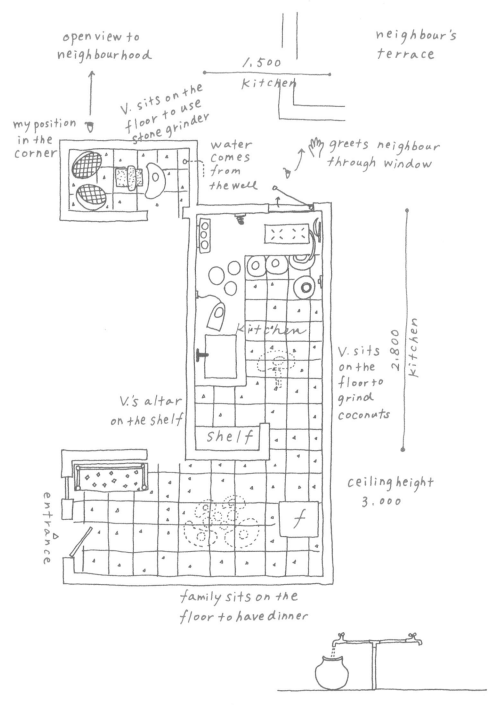

open view to
neighbourhood

neighbour's
terrace

1.500
kitchen

V. sits on the
floor to use
stone grinder

my position
in the
corner

water
comes
from
the well

greets neighbour
through window

Kitchen

V. sits
on the
floor to
grind
coconuts

2.800
kitchen

V.'s altar
on the shelf

Shelf

ceiling height
3.000

entrance

family sits on the
floor to have dinner

outside apartment, there is a water pipe
on the road; water supplied by Chennai city
government, used for cooking and drinking.

K L
I A
T B
C O
H U
E R
N S

3 plastic water vessels in the kitchen.
V. takes water from water pipe outside
every morning.

V. LIVES ON THE SECOND FLOOR with her husband and their two daughters. It is evening, around 5.30 pm, when I arrive at V.'s place. I'm in time to see dinner being prepared. I can tell this entire apartment is like a large family house. All doors open onto corridors.

V. is in the kitchen, waiting for us. Her husband M. is a master printer, who works in the print workshop of our publishing house. Their apartment consists of a bedroom, a kitchen and a narrow living room, which connects the other two rooms. Her two daughters tag along behind her. They smile at us, but then run away. They are very pretty little girls, hair cut very short in the same style, in colourful clothes.

I am told that the batter for the main dish this evening is ready. We are to have *kuzhi paniyaram*, fried dumplings made from rice and *dal* ground together, then allowed to ferment. V. tells us that she has added chopped onions and green pepper to the batter, as she carefully pours it into a special metal pan which has small hollows for the dough (the Tamil word for 'hollow' is *kuzhi*). She has greased each of these hollows with oil, before pouring in the dough. Kuzhi paniyaram reminds me of *takoyaki* ('Octopus Ball'), a favourite snack in Japan. As the dumplings cook, V. dribbles more oil on to each of them. I can see that they actually are almost fried in oil, but very gradually. From time to time, V. takes a small knife and rolls the dumplings about to make sure they brown properly on all sides.

I see a lady looking in through the window near the gas stove. I greet her.

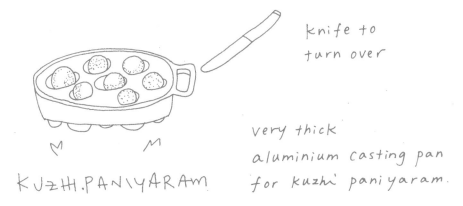

knife to
turn over

KUZHI.PANIYARAM

very thick
aluminium casting pan
for kuzhi paniyaram.

V. winnows peanuts to
get rid of skin.

Meanwhile V. starts to prepare peanut chutney, a relish to go with kuzhi paniyaram. She's roasted whole peanuts already. She takes a straw winnow hanging on the wall, fills it with peanuts, and rubs them together until the skin comes off. Roasting peanuts, cooling, and then removing their skin–for me, this seems a very long process.

V. sits down on the floor with a thump. She has an *arivalmannai*– the traditional cutting and grating tool–in front of her, and begins to grate the flesh of half a coconut into fluffy white scrapings. Then she gets up, reaches outside and snaps a twig of curry leaves off the slender branch of a young curry leaf tree. Peanuts, coconut, and curry leaves are tossed into a bowl, along with roasted *channa dal*, red chillis, garlic, tamarind and salt.

She tells me that she normally uses an electric blender to grind chutney but today she has decided to prepare it with her *ammi*, a traditional stone grinder. She says that she uses it from time to time. The ammi is outside, on the balcony, so V. moves there with the chutney ingredients and a bowl of water. She walks through the bedroom to get to the balcony. It's tiny, but it offers a view of the neighbour's house. I see a chair in a corner and decide to climb onto it–to position myself in such a way that I can see what V. is doing.

V. lowers herself onto the floor in front of the ammi–a flat slightly rough stone with a cylindrical stone like a rolling pin–and washes it clean. I notice that V. doesn't sweep the floor before sitting down. I can tell that the balcony is not considered an outside space, but flows out of the inner rooms. V. puts the chutney mix on the grinding stone, moistens it with a bit of water and begins to roll the stone cylinder on it, up and down, crushing and blending the ingredients into each other. She stops only to scoop the mix under the roller, and add a bit of water.

'AMMI'
stone grinder

water

ingredients

V. ground all ingredients for chutney
by stone grinder. 'Tastes different
from the one you make with mixie.' M. said.

Stainless steel container for coriander and curry leaves in the kitchen.

It's hard work, I think, to grind chutney this way, slowly, adding water as you go along. But V. is cool and collected, getting on with her work.

Her husband M. joins us on the balcony. 'Chutney tastes different when she grinds it on an ammi,' he says with a smile. The heavy grate of stone on stone continues for a while. I am excited, as I see the ingredients blending together into a textured paste, turning into chutney. V. scrapes the paste off expertly with her hands from all stone surfaces, and scoops it into a bowl. This takes time, but I love watching her do this. She doesn't leave even a tiny bit of paste behind on the stone. I see the laborious process that goes into preparing chutney this way. There is a tub in a corner of the balcony, filled with water from the well. V. carefully washes out the ammi and the floor with water.

Then she returns to the kitchen to season the chutney. Mustard seeds, *urad dal* and curry leaves are thrown into sizzling oil, fried and added to the mix. When it is tempered, the chutney looks defined, and is ready to go, as a dish.

We sit on the sofa in the living room, and eat kuzhi paniyaram and peanut chutney. I ask M. where they normally eat their dinner. He points to the floor in front of the refrigerator: 'We eat there.' It's an empty space between the television and the sofa.

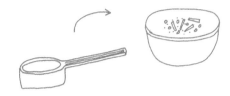

seasoning chutney with fried mustard at the very end.

Winnow
and dosa pan
by the window.

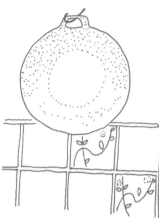

As I understand the cooking process in this house, I experience an enrichment within myself. There is the same expansion of space in V.'s kitchen – much like Aunty S.'s – which continues from the counter to the floor, all the way to the balcony, and to the outside. V. tells me that she goes out into the street to fetch drinking water from the municipal pump. She fills four large vessels, and that means four trips, to-and-fro from her kitchen to the road, every morning.
It must be hard work, and I have seen how lightly V. handles her chores. This ease makes me see the kitchen space as expansive, happily taking in the city itself. I imagine women in their colourful saris, gathering every morning at the communal water pump, chatting as they fill water. I regularly see such sights in the city. To me, they make for a comforting view in some ways, compared to the modern kitchen. It may be fully equipped, but it also encloses people into the kitchen space.

V.'s Verkadalai Chutney
Peanut Chutney

For 6 people

1 cup peanuts, roasted
    and without skin
1/2 cup roasted channa dal
1/4 coconut
5 dried red chillis, or to taste
a marble-sized ball of tamarind
few curry leaves
4 cloves of garlic
salt to taste
1 tbsp. oil
1 tbsp. mustard seeds
1 tbsp. urad dal

Soak tamarind in water until it softens and squeeze out the pulp. Put all the ingredients into a blender and whizz until it's smooth. If you want the chutney to have more texture, blend in short bursts until you have the consistency you want. To temper the chutney, heat oil in a shallow frying pan, put in the mustard seeds and urad dal. Wait until the seeds pop and the dal turns golden. Add it to the chutney.

If you want to make it with kuzhi paniyaram, see p.146 for the recipe.

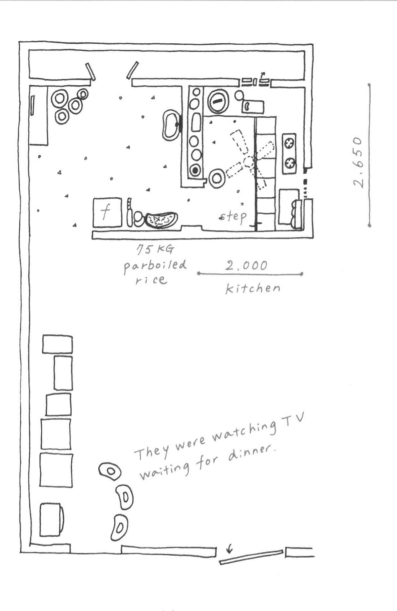

2.650

75 KG
parboiled
rice

2.000
kitchen

step

They were watching TV
waiting for dinner.

tub on the street
for drinking water

KITCHEN WITH MANY HANDS

beautiful entrance
to
kitchen

• interior •

white tiles

kadapa (black stone):

table top

concrete shelf

when you enter kitchen

'COOKING IS THE FIRST THING THAT YOU LEARN when you come to our workshop' says A., who runs the handmade book-printing workshop which belongs to our publishing house. The workshop is special. More than twenty craftsmen, who work at screen-printing and hand-binding, live together here and also cook together. Bachelor workers live on the first floor of a building they share with A. who founded this enterprise. A. lives on the second floor with his family. 'At first we had just one floor. The printing workshop was on the terrace. We lived in the floor below. But over the last twenty years, we've built up the place. Today the workshop is separate from the house, in another building,' A. explains.

I have visited the printing workshop many times—I always found a reason to go there! I love the place. It is such a beautiful and energising experience that I never get bored seeing it. I assume it is hard work to print several overlays of colour as intricately as they do—but they keep calm when they work. And as they print on, the freshly printed sheets mount on the wooden drying racks. Some workers wear aprons and if you look carefully, you can see that they are printed over with images from some of the books they work on!

I visit the place at 7.00 pm one evening, in time to see the workers preparing their dinner. That day, M. is in charge of the cooking that day. Each of the workers takes turns to cook: breakfast, lunch, tea, and dinner. I enter the house, and walk past people who are relaxing after work, watching television. In front of the kitchen there is a small room containing a sack of rice, vessels, and plastic pots to store drinking water. As I enter the kitchen, I see M. start work. The first thing that catches my eye is a huge electric rice cooker. The jute sack of rice in the store room holds 75 kilos of parboiled rice, I'm told, and they eat one and a half sackfuls of rice each month. Wow.

Dinner tonight is rice with bitter-gourd curry. On weekdays, I hear, it is curry and rice for dinner. On weekends – and whenever they have time for cooking – they make chicken curry.

'You must like cooking' I say to M. His way of going about it says it all. 'Yes, I do. I learnt it from my mother, when I lived at home, in the village.' He splits a bitter-gourd into two, and removes the seeds. He slices onions and chops tomatoes. The vegetables are soon in a pot on the stove.

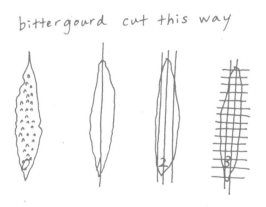
bittergourd cut this way

wooden stick
to crush garlic

I see that M. has measured out seven cups of rice to put into the cooker. He has also already soaked dry tamarind in water in a bowl—he must have done this when he began cooking. As I watch, he begins to knead the soaked tamarind with his fingers, squeezing out the pulp to extract juice. He puts the pulp aside and pours the liquid out into the pot on the stove. He fills the bowl with more water, and kneads the tamarind again. He repeats this a couple of times. After he has squeezed out as much juice as he can, the tamarind looks like a sponge that has dried out.

'What is your favourite dish, Mr. M.?' I ask. He is quiet, and I ask this question to get him to talk. 'Bitter-gourd curry'. His answer makes me happy. 'Thank you very much for cooking your favourite dish today.' Bitter-gourd curry takes forty minutes to cook. 'On a weekday' says M. 'Whoever is cooking needs to spend around thirty to fourty-five minutes on it.'

Later, when I chat with A. about M.'s kitchen, I tell him what I noticed about M. making tamarind juice—that Tamil people use their hands a lot, when they cook. 'We say that good cooking has to do with *kai pakkuvam*,' he replies, using a Tamil phrase. 'I don't know how to translate it into English. It means that the cook's hands define the taste of the dish. A cook has to be 'hand-perfect'!'

Hands are central to cooking and eating in South India. They are needed for both activities. In M.'s kitchen, I discovered one essence of Tamil cooking, something that would come up on other occasions and in other kitchens. The essence of cooking is to be found not just in a family kitchen, but equally in a shared kitchen, like the one at the workshop. Later, I would find this again in a school kitchen, with teachers and students. It is a beautiful thing, the closeness that they shared. It surprised me, if I am to be honest. It was a learning process for me—to understand the distance between me and the people I met. At the same time, I admired what they had.

cup
plate

water for cooking
from water supply pipe
outside the house.

• M's bitter gourd curry + rice •

- small onions
- tomato
- garlic
- bittergourd ① ② ③ cut this way

② all veggies

cut veggies on the plate

 oil ① spices

 spice case

③ on fire for a while ④ tamarind

water

dried
tamarind

squeeze
tamarind juice

M.'s Pavakkai Karakulambu
Bitter-gourd Curry

For 8 people

5 small onions
2 large dried red chillies
3 tomatoes
3 large bitter-gourds
10 garlic cloves
a small ball of tamarind
2 tbsp. mustard seeds
3 tbsp. urad dal
5 tbsp. sambar powder
    (spice mix, available in South
    Indian grocery stores) or curry
    powder
salt to taste
3–4 tbsp. oil

Soak the tamarind in water – this will soften the tamarind and help you squeeze out the juice from it. Slice the onions, and chop tomatoes in cubes. Cut the bitter-gourds into halves, and remove the seeds. Chop them up into small pieces. Crush garlic pods into a bowl, using a wooden ladle. Then heat the oil in a heavy bottomed pot. Once it begins to sizzle, throw in mustard seeds and the red chillies, and when they pop, add the *urad dal*. When the urad dal turns golden, add the chopped onions, tomatoes, garlic and bitter-gourd. Saute until the vegetables soften. Now add *sambar* powder, salt and tamarind juice and bring to a boil.

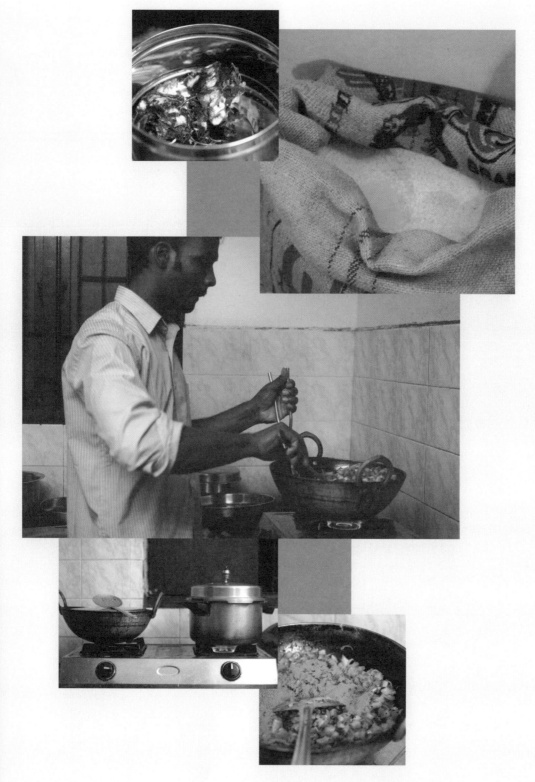

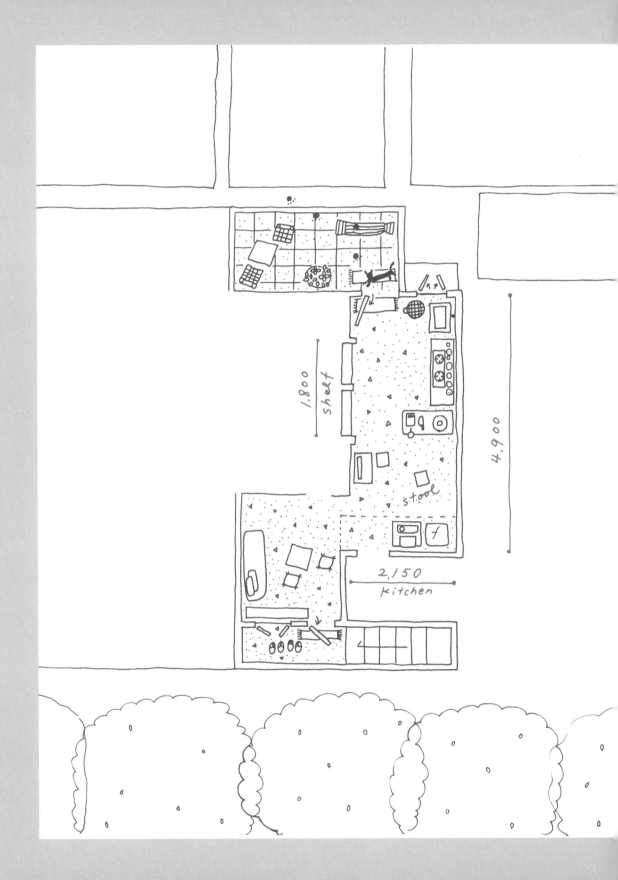

1,800
shelf

4,900

stool

2,150
kitchen

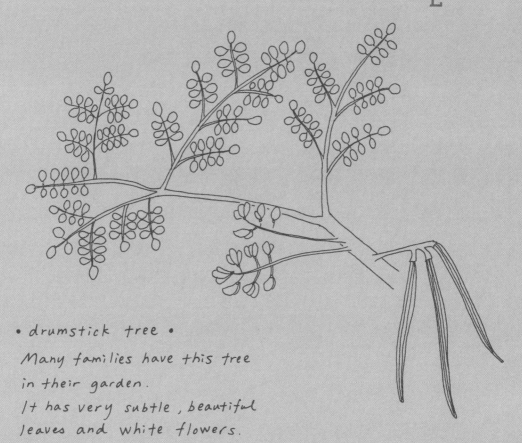

KITCHEN WITH A STOOL

• drumstick tree •
Many families have this tree
in their garden.
It has very subtle, beautiful
leaves and white flowers.

N. AND S. ARE A BRITISH-INDIAN COUPLE. N. is a graphic designer and S. is a social science researcher. They live in a small apartment shaded by large trees. To get there, you have to go past an old and well-known school for traditional dance, down a wide empty road, and then turn into a small path that leads you to the quiet street that fronts their apartment. It is as if you are visiting a hidden world.

N. and S.'s home is on the first floor of a two-storey house. Their landlord's family lives on the ground floor. Since they are vegetarian, they don't want their tenants to cook meat or fish either and so N. and S. have to cook vegetarian food in their house. This is the first time I've heard something like this.

Their home is a small cosy place with a living room, a bedroom and a kitchen. The kitchen opens out into a large terrace which is ringed on all sides by tall apartments. A quiet place in the middle of the city. The door to the terrace from the kitchen is always open. Cats that belong to their neighbours stroll in and sleep by the kitchen door.

When I first arrived in Chennai, before this project took shape, their home was the first local house that I visited. It was night-time. I sat on a stool, and we chatted as they cooked. Though it was 'winter' in Chennai, it was warm enough to leave the windows and doors open, even at night. I felt good and special, because I had flown in from Tokyo where winter had just begun.

This is the second time that I am visiting them. It is past noon and N. has just come home from her morning class, where she is learning Tamil. S. is on a professional video-call.

'Do you think you could make *idli* for lunch?' I ask, remembering how tasty it is. Idli is a characteristic Tamil dish and perhaps one of the oldest fermented foods in the world. Idlis are made from a special kind of batter of rice and *dal* ground together, and left to ferment overnight. The dough rises because of natural bacteria, without any yeast being added. Idli batter is poured into special steaming pans with small hollows. People eating idli from small stalls on the road is a common morning sight in Tamil Nadu. It is breakfast food.

'Idli batter is usually made at home. That's how you're supposed to do it!' exclaims S. as he takes out a ready-made packet of batter from a shopping bag. I sit on the same stool that I had sat on earlier, at the entrance to the kitchen. I feel this had become my regular position in this house.

S. and N. want to cook drumstick *sambar* (a typical Tamil stew), and make mint and coconut chutney to go with the idli. A drumstick (moringa, called *murungaikai* in Tamil) is a slender long green pod with a thick fibrous skin. The edible part inside consists of white, delicate flesh and seeds. I've never seen anything like it before. The drumstick tree is very common in this part of the world and many Tamil families have one in their yard. Drumstick sambar tastes very special, and many Tamil friends tell me it is their favourite sambar.

Both N. and S. get busy around the kitchen. I notice that S., the Indian part of the couple, is in charge – since this is an Indian meal. S. is a rather precise cook. He cuts the drumsticks into identical sized pieces. He then chops a white radish – also for the sambar – into beautifully even slices. The chopped vegetables are then arranged on a plate.

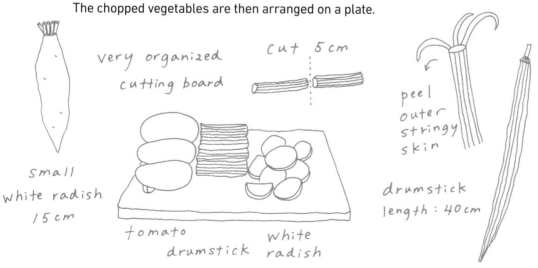

very organized
cutting board

cut 5cm

peel
outer
stringy
skin

small
white radish
15cm

tomato
drumstick

white
radish

drumstick
length : 40cm

drumstick
tomatoes
masoor dal
tamarind juice
turmeric powder
— all at once!

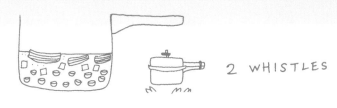

2 WHISTLES

I'm always fascinated by the vivid colours of vegetables here. Tomatoes are red and transparent. Mint is a deep green, and onions – especially when shot through with sunlight – are a translucent purple and white.

'I have my own way of cooking,' says S. 'When I was young and lived at home, I just ate, I didn't help in the kitchen. Mother always cooked for us.' He keeps talking as he works. 'I take lots of short-cuts when I cook.'

I see him put the drumsticks and dal in a vessel, cover them with tamarind juice and place the whole thing inside a pressure cooker. I discover later that this is not how it is usually done – you stew the vegetables in tamarind juice on low heat, then add the cooked dal later.

But seeing his 'short-cut' method, I realize that he has actually condensed several processes into one, and that this is indeed possible in Tamil cooking. I feel confident that I too can cook a Tamil dish soon.

N. has lived in Sri Lanka for a year, which is perhaps why their kitchen shows a bit of Sri Lankan influence: for instance, they use only coconut oil for cooking. There is also a coconut grater that she has brought back from Sri Lanka – you hold a coconut half against the grater blade and turn a handle. Fresh coconut is an essential ingredient in the Tamil kitchen as well. After all, the flight to Sri Lanka just takes an hour from Chennai.

'We must have fresh chutney' says N., starting to grind mint in a blender.

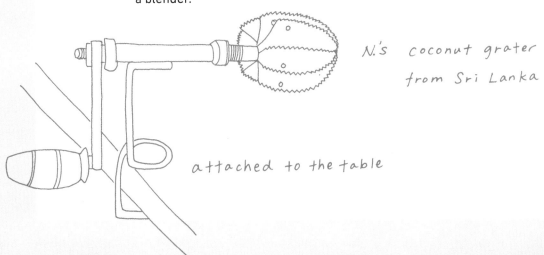

N.'s coconut grater
from Sri Lanka

attached to the table

'Two chutneys! Fancy lunch!' S. announces soon. He's busy popping
mustard seeds in a pan. 'It's a sort of tempering for sambar. You add
it at the end. I usually skip this part, but not today,' he adds.

Four dishes in an hour!

We have lunch in the living room. Time passes quickly and
a colleague comes by to pick me up. We're going to go to the
northern part of the city, to a wholesale paper mart to buy some
cardboard I need for a project.

For me, this seems normal, part of my everyday life, to have lunch
with friends and then return to work. But my everyday now is in
a new city and invariably, there's always a special moment lying in
wait for me. This is such a moment, when my life shifts a bit, and
I find myself becoming part of the city.

As I leave N. and S.'s home, I know this is only the beginning –
they've become my friends, and I will visit their kitchen many times.
And from the beginning, I have marked out my special seat, the stool
at the entrance to their kitchen. It captures their attitude, their way
of inviting people into their place. When you sit on the stool, you get
to view the entire kitchen, which is actually a narrow strip of space,
modelled on what I understand to be a fairly typical Indian kitchen
plan. I feel I am allowed to watch and be part of this space.

fry other ingredients

S. & N. use
coconut oil
for all cooking

S.'s Murungaikai Sambar
Stew with Drumsticks

For 4 people

1 drumstick
3 tomatoes
2 onions
1 large white radishes
1/2 cup masoor dal
a lemon-sized ball of tamarind
1 tbsp. mustard seeds
1 tbsp. sambar powder
salt to taste
1 tsp. coconut oil
a sprig of coriander

Soak tamarind in water. After it has soaked for around half an hour, squeeze out the juice into a cup. Chop all the vegetables. Then put the vegetables, *masoor dal* and tamarind into a vessel, add sambar powder and salt, and cook in a pressure cooker. (You can also boil them together in a pot, if you don't have a pressure cooker). Heat the coconut oil in a small frying pan, add mustard seeds and wait until they pop. Pour this tempering over the sambar.

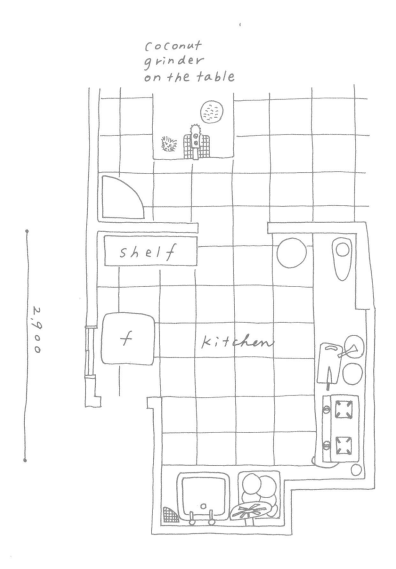

coconut
grinder
on the table

shelf

+ kitchen

2,900

3.250

B
I
L
I
N
G
U
A
L

K
I
T
C
H
E
N

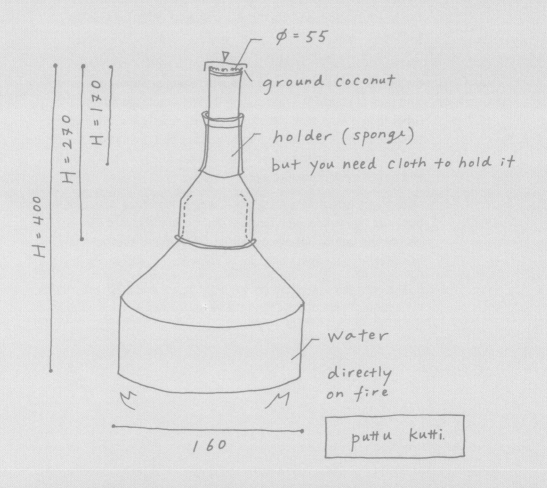

ø = 55

ground coconut

holder (sponge)
but you need cloth to hold it

water

directly
on fire

H = 400

H = 270

H = 170

160

puttu kutti.

coconut oil

stir fried

① ② ③ ④ ⑤

- kadala curry -
(chickpea)

●●●●
① onion x 3

garlic x 4

ginger

② heaped
spoon
of spices

chilli
coriander
fennel
turmeric

'HAVE YOU EVER THOUGHT ABOUT MOVING CLOSER TO THE OFFICE? It must be hard, commuting this long distance every day.' I ask S., who is in charge of Finance at our publishing house. We are in an autorickshaw, on our way to his house. S. has just finished work. We're in rush hour traffic – the road packed with cars, autos and motorbikes – and conversing in the middle of this chaos.

'Of course I would like to. But we want to stay in our current apartment since a lot of people from Kerala live there.'

S. is Muslim. Sometimes I see him praying on the floor in his office space, kneeling on a small carpet. He was born in a town on the border between Tamil Nadu and Kerala, and he went to a university in Kerala. He tells me that he wanted to become a doctor, like his father. But somehow he ended up becoming an accountant.

The talk turns to food. 'Are there any special rules for Muslim kitchens?' I ask.

'Not really, except that we eat halal meat, which is meat treated the proper way. I'm in charge of buying meat at home,' he replies. 'And then of course we fast during the month of Ramadhan. Other than that, it is all a matter of taste. Initially, my wife cooked brown rice. But I couldn't bring myself to like it. So I asked her if she would mind shifting over to white rice. She got used to that, and now we eat white rice every day.'

I had a very nice time getting to know S. In the office he is quietly busy – so I somehow didn't expect that he would talk to me about his life and family. But during our long ride in the autorickshaw, I discovered a lot about him, got to know his life story in fact.

It takes an hour and a half for us to get to S.'s place. We travel from the southern side of the city to the west. S. lives with his wife, Sh., their two daughters, and S.'s mother. Sh. has beautiful black hair and a gentle expression in her large eyes. S.'s mother is busy, taking care of his younger daughter, who is still a baby.

I'm greeted with a glass of juice. Soon Sh. begins to cook.

She says that she cooks part of the dinner earlier in the day, soon after she takes her daughter to school in the morning. 'That's the only free time I have.' When her daughter comes home, Sh. has to help with her homework. They have dinner at 9.30 pm when S. comes back home, and the entire family eats together. 'In the morning, I cook everything for dinner except *chapati* which I make fresh, just before we sit down to dinner.'

Today, she has shifted her cooking time because of me. Dinner is to be *kadala* curry (chickpea curry), *payaru* (cooked green gram) and *puttu* (steamed rice and coconut roll). I'm told that this is typical Kerala food.

③ MASALA
   clove
   cardamom
   cinnamon

Sh. starts with the kadala curry. She fries sliced onions, garlic and ginger in a shallow pan. I notice that she uses coconut oil. Then she reaches for a container with four different spice powders: chilli, coriander, turmeric and fennel. Soon there is a little spice mountain sizzling in the pan. To this she adds *garam masala* powder (a spice mix available in shops), and tosses in a few cloves, cardamoms and a stick of cinnamon. Slit green chillies and a few curry leaves come next, along with the cooked chickpeas. A sweet fragrance, of a kind that I have never encountered before, fills the kitchen.

④ chickpea
   3 whistles

   pressure
   cooker

I discover that there are three basic ingredients for a Kerala meal: coconut, coconut oil and black pepper. Sh. gets fresh supplies of these from her mother, who sends her a package every month, harvested from her own garden in Kerala. I ask S. what tools he and his family would want on a desert island, should they ever

⑤ fresh green
     chilli

1

all
home-
made

- coconut
- coconut oil
- curry leaves

always from
S.'s mother in Kerala

find themselves on one. He smiles and says, '"*Puttu kutti*" (a puttu steamer) and a coconut grinder!' Perhaps Sh.'s mother will send her a package, even to a desert island!

Puttu is a steamed dish made with rice flour and grated coconut. Sh. is now ready to make it. She holds a coconut in one hand, and with the other, reaches under the kitchen sink and – to my surprise – brings out a machete. I am startled at the picture she makes: a young woman swinging a large machete in the middle of her kitchen! She looks quite fierce.

Coconut
from S.'s
mom

Sh. swipes at the coconut in her hand with the machete, and like magic, splits it into two halves. She takes them into the dining area, where there is a coconut grater screwed onto the edge of the table. She grates the coconut, then starts to fill the puttu kutti: first with thick and crumbly and somewhat wet rice flour (she's already mixed rice flour with water to make this crumble), and then a layer of grated coconut. She alternates rice crumble and coconut until the kutti is filled, then closes and places it on the stove, to steam.

I look around the kitchen and see that the tiles are stuck with images of different fruits. Sh. has made these stickers herself, and I notice how they add to the ambience of her kitchen. She doesn't speak much English, and so we don't really converse, but from her actions, I can see that she is a calm person. She stayed cool even when she had to wield that machete. And now, she's calmly slicing onions with a swirling tool that is activated with a string, using centrifugal action. It's like a toy.

iron

coconut
machete

'Dinner is ready,' says Sh. as she prepares to lay the plates. The plates are patterned to look like banana leaves. 'Maybe you need a spoon?' she says, and offers me one.

'First you eat puttu with payaru – that's mild. Next you move to kadala curry, that's going to be spicy,' S. explains. 'Between the mild and

spicy, help yourself to some banana and sugar!' That's when I see
that Sh. has put out banana slices and some sugar. The puttu tastes
wonderful, slightly sweet, filled with the mixed aroma of coconut
and spices, alternating with sugar and banana.

'Puttu is C.'s favourite dish,' says S. C. is their elder daughter.
She shows me her drawings of vegetables. Her grandmother is still
with her little sister, chatting away to the baby. Her chatter seems
like music to me. Sh. explains to me – in Tamil and Malayalam, with
S. translating for us – what goes into each of the dishes she has made.

I feel cosy and safe. Maybe due to the time of day? Or is it the warm
light in the kitchen that makes me feel that way? There is a slight
sense of being away from home, but being connected to this place.
Kerala is a constant reference, even though the family speaks Tamil
as well. C. studies Tamil at school and they talk in Malayalam at
home. I see how their kitchen straddles two places, reflecting the
life they lead.

• How to eat the 'Malayalam' way •

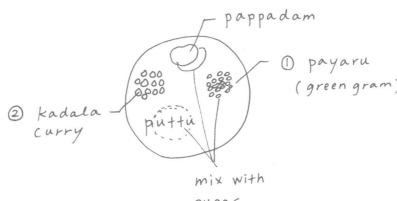

1. eat payaru first.
   mix puttu, pappadam, payaru and sugar.

① 'puttu, banana and sugar
② kadala curry and puttu

S.'s Puttu
Steamed Rice and Coconut Rolls

For 6 people

rice flour
1 coconut
water

Mix rice flour with water, until you get a mixture that is crumbly and slightly wet. Grate the coconut. Start filling the puttu kutti with rice crumble and coconut, alternating between the two. Place the puttu kutti without its lid on the stove. When it starts steaming, close it. Reduce the heat, and let the puttu steam for around three minutes. Take it off the stove. Allow the puttu kutti to cool a little. Then carefully lever the puttu out from the kutti, with a knife. One roll of puttu makes one serving.

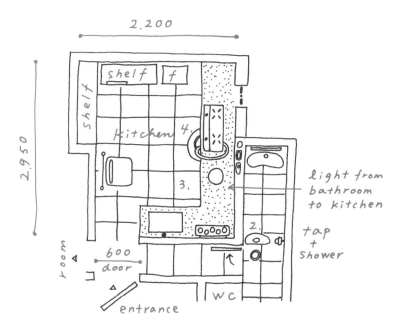

2.200

2.950

shelf

shelf   f

shelf

Kitchen 4.

3.

light from
bathroom
to kitchen

2.

tap
+
shower

room

600
door

entrance

WC

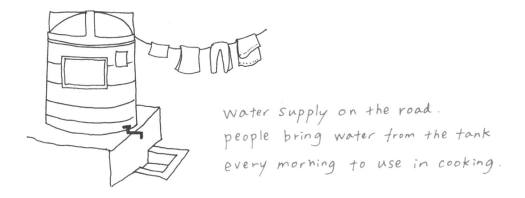

Water supply on the road.
people bring water from the tank
every morning to use in cooking.

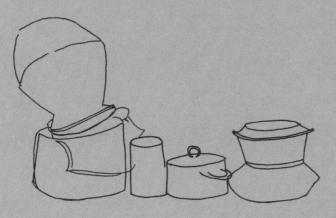

kitchen vessels

Fishing village amongst the oldest areas in
Chennai existed before British colonisation.
Fishing village now in the center of the city.

R.'S HOME IS IN A FISHING VILLAGE in the centre of Chennai. The city only came into being in the 17th century, when it was developed as a British colonial town. Before this, the area was a string of fishing villages, and people of the fisher community were the original inhabitants of the place. Even in today's Chennai, the coastline is dotted with fishing villages, which continue to exist even as they are surrounded by the expanding city. R. grew up in such a village, and continues to live there. He works in our publishing house, and is in charge of packing and dispatching books.

Sunday morning: I am riding pillion on R.'s motorbike, heading to the village. We drive for about fifteen minutes, until we come to the sea. Along the coastline, I see women sitting on the ground, selling fish from makeshift stands and tables. People from all over the city come here to buy fresh fish.

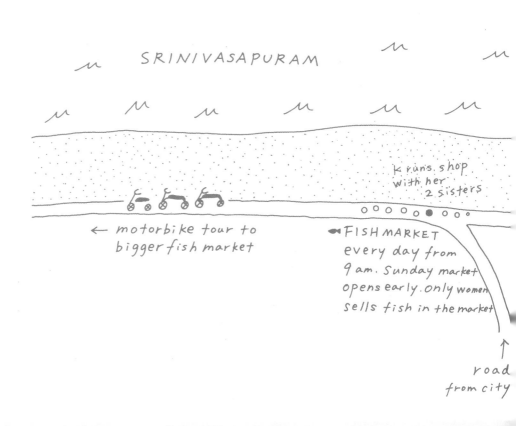

SRINIVASAPURAM

k runs shop
with her
2 sisters

← motorbike tour to
bigger fish market

◄FISH MARKET
every day from
9 am. Sunday market
opens early. only women
sells fish in the market

↑
road
from city

R.'s mother K. runs such a shop, along with her two sisters. She displays her fish on a plywood board balanced on large baskets. The fish on offer are small, fresh, and beautiful. *Aji* (mackerel), *Katsuo* (tuna)... the fish here look very similar to what I eat back in Japan, and I'm pleased.

The sisters attend to their customers: they're happy to clean and cut the fish if needed. K. keeps busy, peeling and de-veining shrimp. Her hands are constantly moving, always at work. I see three men standing behind her, smiling and talking. R. introduces them as his friends.

Boys play cricket on the beach. 'Sunday scene.' says R. More of his friends come by on their motorbikes and stop near K.'s shop. I am introduced to all of them. R. says, 'Let's visit my sister!'

And so we go to R.'s sister RA.'s house, six of us on four motorbikes. Her home is part of a tenement on the beach. RA. offers us a snack: wheat *upma* (a savory grain dish) and *chai*. We then move on to

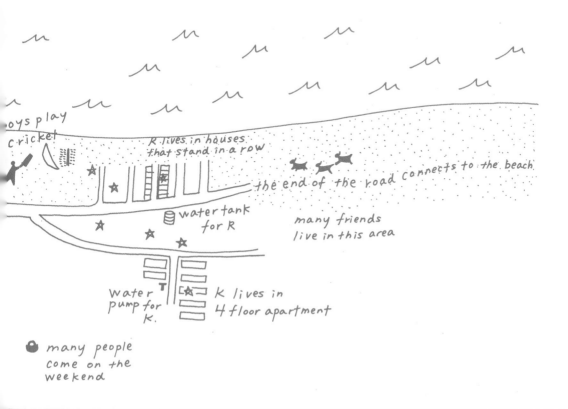

another fish market at the other end of the long beach, taking RA.'s two year-old daughter with us. It begins to rain, and we hurry back to R.'s mother's place. Lunch has been cooked and is waiting for us.

But before we eat, K. goes out again to fetch another fish, just to show me how she fries it. In the end, lunch turns out to be a luxurious affair: fish gravy, shrimp gravy, fish fry and rice. After making sure that all of us are eating well, K. starts on her own lunch. Just then, RA.'s four-year old son comes in. K. begins to make balls of rice, rolling them skillfully between the fingers and palm of one hand. She tosses a rice ball into her mouth… and another into her grandson's mouth. I'm surprised at how big these rice balls are–each of them is the size of a small *onigiri*, the Japanese rice ball we usually have for lunch. The child has to swallow one ball, before he gets the next, and in between he bites into a piece of fried fish that he clutches in his hand. When he has a moment to pause, he says, 'I don't want anymore.' But he is coaxed to eat more–some of the older boys tell him that he must eat up. After making sure that all is well with us, K. gets back to work at her fish shop.

K. is a tough mother, but she's very kind. I look around and notice her altar. It is an interesting place: it has pictures of Jesus with Maria,

• fish for the day •

squid in water.

sisters sit in front selling, cutting and cleaning fishes

sillaginidae   shrimp

big fish under the cloth

squid

crab
barracudda
shark

and also some Hindu gods. Since Hindus worship many gods, maybe it is easy for a Hindu to accept one more god as their own? The image remains in my mind: two gods from two different religions next to each other in her altar. The image speaks of K.'s generosity.

rice container

In a while, I start to wonder whether I should leave, but R. and his friends are in no hurry, they're watching TV switching between a Tamil soap and an English movie. So I stay on. K. returns in a while, and takes a nap in the same room. We spend the whole afternoon watching TV and drinking juice. I am happily there, and thank them all for letting me stay.

At night, when I get back, I think about their hospitality. At RA.'s place, when chai was ready, it was served to everyone who was there. So was the fish gravy at K.'s house. RA.'s family lives in one room with a cooking space in one corner; and K. lives in a tiny apartment with one room and a kitchen. The kitchens are small in size, but they are open to all, to friends, and kin, and to visitors like me. I realise something: the more kitchens are open to other people, the larger they become.

I had spent the day with R. and his friends, and during the entire time, people kept dropping in: his friend's daughter, his cousin, some neighbours. And in the middle of all this, daily life continued: children were bathed, their clothes changed, a daughter's hair was combed... it all happened easily, in a flow, and I was effortlessly in the middle of the everyday.

When I think of K.'s kitchen, it strikes me that it's not just the place in which she cooks. Her kitchen includes the whole landscape, the beach, and the sea beyond. This was true of all the places we went to that day – it was the sea which connected all the kitchens I had seen, forming a backdrop to the scenes that unfolded on its shore.

• R's kitchen •

width 1.000

buit-in concrete shelf

depth
300

only porcelain
cups

knives

Serving plates

lunch
boxes

side
dish

H = 460

rice

sambar

idly

fish
curry

dad
gravy

pressure
cooker

H = 630

so many pots !!!

used to be have
handles

• 3 places to prepare and cook seer fish •

1. cut and clean fish
   at fish market

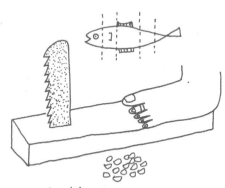

hold

down plank
with foot

2. washing fish

tap

3. marinate fish

masala
powder   ginger & garlic
         paste   salt

4. fried fish

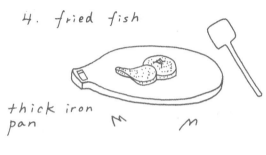

thick iron
pan

K.'s Vanjaram
Fried Seer Fish

For 4 people

1 *vanjaram* fish
2 tbsp ginger and garlic paste
1 tbsp. masala powder
    (ready-made spice found in
    grocery stores)
salt to taste
a couple of tbsps. oil

Cut the fish into slices and clean them. Coat each slice with *masala* powder, ginger and garlic paste, and salt. (Ginger and garlic paste is usually pre-prepared and kept ready as seasoning; it could also be bought in shops.) Allow the fish to marinate for a while. Coat a flat griddle with oil and heat thoroughly. Shallow fry the fish slices in batches. Turn down the flame after they brown on both sides, and cook until done through.

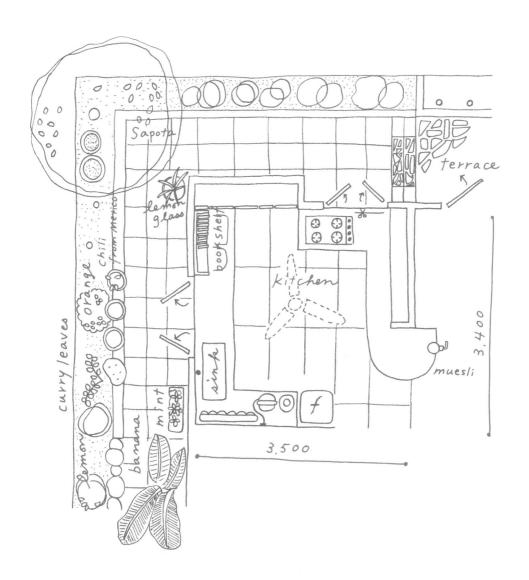

Sapota

terrace

lemon
glass

bookshelf

curry leaves

chili

from mexico

orange

lemon

banana

mint

sink

kitchen

muesli

f

3,400

3,500

K I T C H E N
W O R L D S

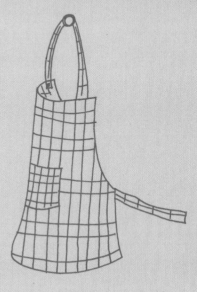

G. is the only one
who wore an apron.

G. IS THE HEAD OF OUR PUBLISHING HOUSE. She is the one who invited me to Chennai, and ever since I arrived here, I have been eating lunch with her every day at our workplace. Lunch time is not long, but it is intense. We talk a lot, as we share each other's food. I've learned a great deal about Tamil food at our lunch table, through tasting as well as listening. I know that G. has a great passion for cooking, and has evolved her own philosophy of food, taste and nutrition. She cooks regularly, mostly during the weekend. During the working week, she employs a cook.

G.'s home is close to the sea. She lives in an apartment with her husband and son. For me, reaching her kitchen is an adventure – not because it's far away, but because it's the first time that I take an autorickshaw by myself through the city. So I'm really relieved when I find myself at her doorstep, ringing the bell.

sapota

G.'s home is on the ground floor of a four-storey building. I enter and am immediately taken to the far end of the house. 'Let me show you the garden.' says G., and walks me to an open terrace. It's paved, with steps leading to small cemented pathways. Both sides of the pathways are planted with trees and bushes.

'It's small, just a space behind the building, but I love it.' says G. It's more than twenty years since she and her family moved in here. Today, her little garden even has fruit trees – lemon, sapota, and guava trees. 'These are chilli plants that I brought back from Mexico. And I'm glad that these curry leaves have finally taken root.' G. walks me through the garden, pointing to various things.

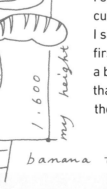

1.600 my height

banana tree

I notice banana trees at one end of a pathway. I smile, realising that the raw bananas in the curry she brings for lunch are from here. I say a silent thank you to the tree – this is the first time in my life that I'm actually seeing a banana tree. This one is smaller and shorter than I imagined. I can reach up and touch the leaves.

This pathway garden surrounds G.'s kitchen. Both the large kitchen windows have views of plants and trees. G.'s kitchen is unlike any of the South Indian kitchens I've visited. Most of them tend to be narrow, usually opening out of the living room, with a window on the other side. But G.'s kitchen space is large and square, open to the dining area. 'This was originally intended to be a bedroom in the architect's plan for the flat,' G. explains. 'The actual kitchen was tucked away on the other side of the living room. We asked for the spaces to be switched, and removed one of the walls to connect the kitchen to the dining area.'

She starts her preparations for lunch, saying 'I love cooking while listening to music. But today I have you, Nao.'

G. has lived in Germany for many years, since her husband is from there. 'I was there in the 1970's and 80's, when the ecological movement started, and I was really interested and influenced by it. I read a lot about the politics of food,' she reminisces. 'There was another thing: I'm a vegetarian, and Germany's meat culture came as quite a shock – a normal meal consisted of large cuts of meat, accompanied by a few overcooked vegetables. As for vegetarian restaurants there were none. So I taught myself to cook.'

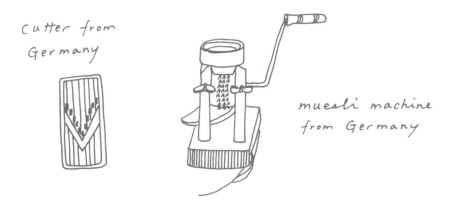

cutter from
Germany

muesli machine
from Germany

G. learned cooking through cookbooks. 'You need to go through
a basic learning period, and follow a written recipe exactly. Once you
understand how food behaves, you can start improvising, which is what
I do now, all the time.' She points to a bowl of sprouts: 'It's tricky to get
lentils to sprout, so I prefer to do it myself.' She opens her microwave
and pushes a bowl of carrots into it. 'When I want to steam carrots
lightly, I microwave them a bit. They stay crisp, but cook through.'
She then takes down a notebook from a bookshelf in the kitchen, and
shows it to me. It's a recipe book written in Tamil, in her mother's
handwriting. 'My mother died when I was thirty-five,' G. explains.
'These are recipes she wrote down for me nearly forty years ago.
Look how beautiful her handwriting is.' I see a young girl inside her
grown-up self.

She carries on cooking as we continue to talk. 'I'm going to make
brown rice...' G. says, pulling out a large electric rice cooker from
a drawer. It's an old one. 'I inherited this from my mother. It's very
simple, just one button: "On/Off".' It's obvious that the cooker is
ancient, enough for the Teflon to have worn off the inner vessel.
I'm strangely thrilled at the sight, it reminds me of a similar cooker
I've seen at a Japanese skiing lodge in the mountains.

G. takes a lemon from the fridge. She's been chopping vegetables
for a salad. She looks for something and finally finds it in a drawer –
a lemon zester. 'One of my very favourite tools. An Italian friend gave
it to me.' It's small and handy, meant for peeling the rind finely off
a lemon. I watch as curls of lemon peel land into the salad.

'Nao, I bought some Miso when I was in Japan, last summer – when
we met.' says G., and shows me a large bag of Miso from the fridge.
Miso is made from fermented soybeans and we add it to our daily
soup. It's a very Japanese ingredient. 'I wanted to buy some when
I went to the local street market in Kyoto. An old woman at the Miso

from her friend
in Italy

rice cooker
from G's mother

spices & soy sauce
from Japan

shop put a huge scoop into a bag and asked me if it was enough.
I told her it was fine, though I had no idea how much I would really
need. So I carried all this Miso back to India, and it's still here.'

Watching her cooking, I realise how much the kitchen contains
of G.'s life. Here is where she collects her fragments of memory
and experience – of her youthful days in Germany, the flavour and
atmosphere of 1970s Europe, the ecological movement, the many
places she has visited and the many friends she has made in
different countries, the memory of her mother... every object here has
a story. Some of them arrived here through choice, and some through
serendipity. That's why her kitchen is such an interesting mix.

When lunch is ready, G.'s husband, son and his girlfriend join us.
We eat goulash with soy nuggets, *basmati* brown rice, cucumber and
carrot salad. G.'s lunch reminds me of a weekend in Finland, where
I have spent many years of my adult life. It makes me feel homesick
for what I consider my second motherland. After lunch, I browse
through G.'s kitchen bookshelf which is filled with cookery books.
A funny yet philosophical title catches my eye: 'Recipes for Small
Planets'. I understand and empathise.

G.'s Bookshelf in the kitchen

G.'s Goulash

For 5 people

500 gms kidney beans
12 tomatoes
3 onions
6 large garlic pods
3 green paprika
3 small potatoes
250 gms. soya nuggets
1 tsp. chilli powder
2 tbsp. paprika powder
2 tbsp. cumin powder
lg tbsp. dried oregano
salt to taste
2 tbsp. olive oil

Soak kidney beans overnight, or for at least three to four hours. Pressure cook them. Soak soya nuggets in hot water for half an hour. Pour boiling water over the tomatoes. Once they are cool enough to handle, slip the skin off the tomatoes and pulp them up roughly. Chop the onion and green peppers. Heat olive oil in a pressure cooker and saute the onions and garlic until they turn brown. Add the spice powders and fry through. Add the green paprika, diced potatoes, cooked kidney beans, soya nuggets, tomatoes and salt. Pressure cook the mixture, adding a bit of olive oil. When the cooker is opened, stir and crush some of the stew with the back of a ladle, to make the goulash thicker. Bring to another boil and then serve.

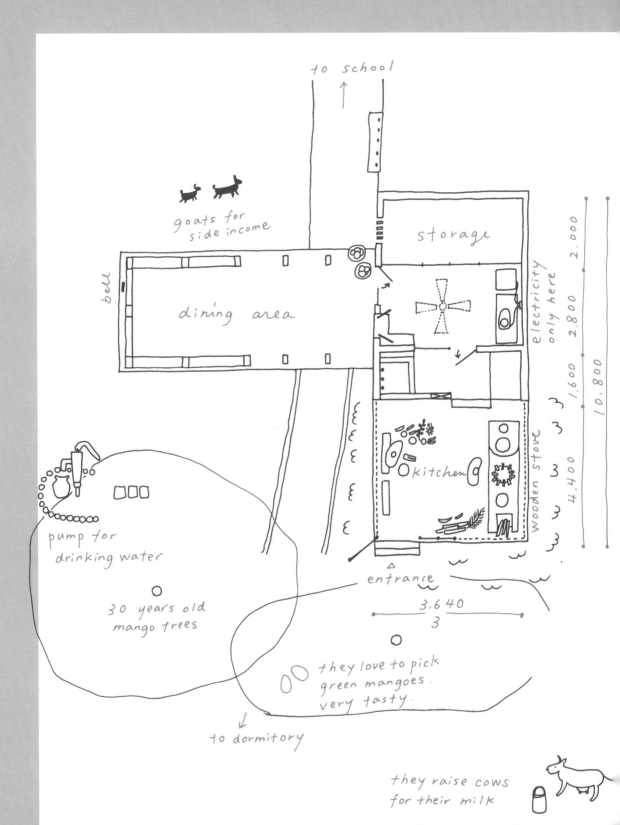

to school

goats for
side income

bell

storage

electricity
only here

dining   area

2.000
2.800
1.600
4.400
10.800

wooden stove

kitchen

pump for
drinking water

30 years old
mango trees

entrance

3.640
3

they love to pick
green mangoes.
very tasty.

to dormitory

they raise cows
for their milk

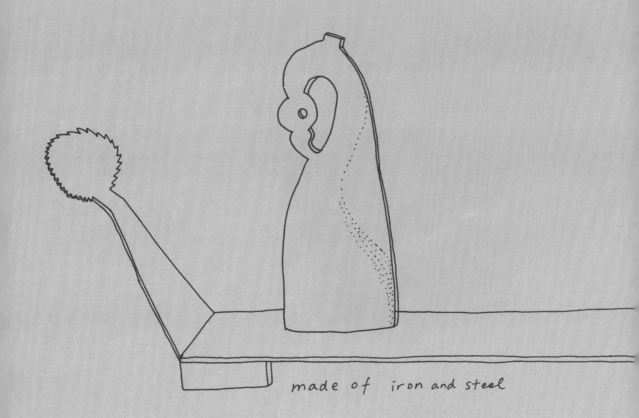

made of iron and steel

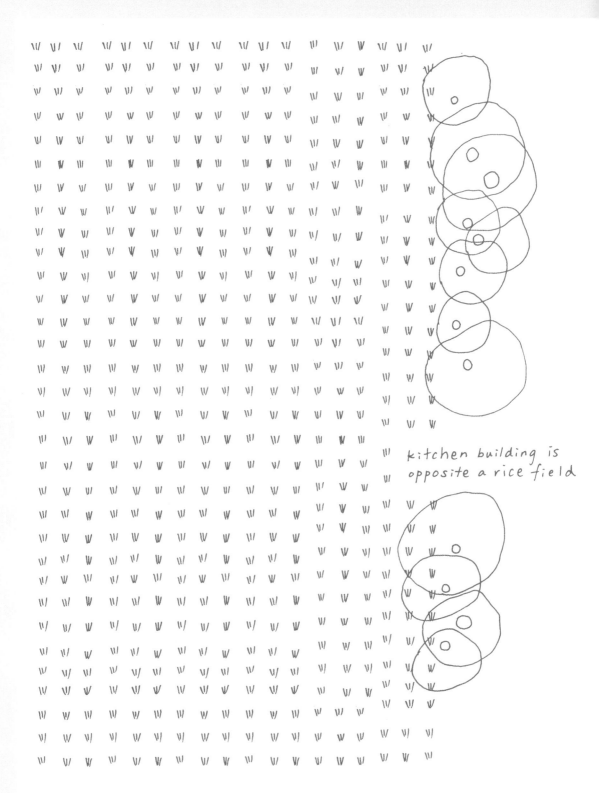

kitchen building is
opposite a rice field

THIS TIME I'M GOING TO VISIT A SCHOOL KITCHEN. The school I am going to is called Vanavil (Rainbow), set up some years ago by R., a young woman I met through mutual friends. I have to go back in time to explain how the school came into being. In 2004, the coast of Tamil Nadu was hit by a huge tsunami, which caused very severe damage to villages all along the coast. The small seaside town of Nagapattinam was particularly affected. R. – who was working for the Tamil film industry at the time – went to Nagapattinam to work as a relief volunteer. This experience changed her life.

One day, as R. and other volunteers were distributing relief material which had come in generously from everywhere, she saw some children begging on the street. R. found that very odd – in a town overflowing with relief goods, why were these children begging? So she talked to them to find out, and learned that they were from a nomadic tribal community. Since they didn't have a stable home, their families were not registered as residents in that town; and unregistered people do not get relief.

R. played with the children for a while, and found out more about them. 'At that time, we were helping to look for bodies of people which were scattered all across the coast,' R. explained to me. 'So being with the children was nice, a bit of a relief.'

But the children's situation was dire. R. discovered that there were forty-two families with children, who had not received any assistance. She decided to help them get relief, and also to find out if something could be done for the kids, many of whom had never been to school. She got the permission to send them to nearby schools, but was immediately faced with the next problem. The children now had a right to education, but they faced a huge learning gap, since they had never been to school.

So she decided to start a bridge school, and called it Vanavil.
The school now has nearly a hundred students aged between
three and sixteen, living and studying there.

This is the Rainbow School that I'm on my way to now, with R. and
her friend S., who is an artist. We take a night train from the Chennai
Egmore Railway Station. At 11.00 pm. the platform is full of people.
A train with darkened windows slides into the platform – and even
before it stops, people start clambering on. We manage to get into the
third class passenger coach. I am a bit nervous. We will be travelling
for eight hours.

We arrive safely the next morning, get off the train and make our
way to the school, which is on the outskirts of a small village near
Nagapattinam. There is only one road to Vanavil from the nearest
village and it's a pretty route, through beautiful rice fields which
stretch as far as the eye can see.

When we reach the school, I discover that the kitchen and dining area
are located at its very centre. They in fact connect the school building
with the dormitory, where the children sleep. The kitchen also opens
onto a rice field – the school cultivates its own rice. There are cows here

vessels for
collecting water

as well, so the school has a ready supply of milk. There is a plan to grow vegetables. 'We want to be as self-sufficient as possible,' R. says.

I find the children mischievous, tough and charming. They run up and surround me, and ask me a hundred questions. They sing the Indian national anthem, and ask me to sing the Japanese one.

We stay at a place nearby, and the next morning, I'm up at 6.00 am, ready to go. I'm to be in the school kitchen at 6.45. It is raining. I wrap my camera in a plastic bag and stow it into my backpack. S. picks me up on his motorbike, and as we ride along, he points to a woman walking in the rain, holding up her umbrella. She is N., their cook. She looks calm.

At school, we go directly to the kitchen. The assistant cook L. is already there, sorting through vegetables. There is also a young girl sitting on the floor and eating. She is breakfasting on the rice left over from the night before. She goes to the local high school. The rain has meanwhile stopped, and morning mist comes down, covering the fields. N. the cook arrives, and their day begins. The first thing they do is to pump water from a hand pump outside, and start filling water into a large plastic container in the kitchen. It takes a while before it is filled up.

axe with wooden handle

Soon children start to come in and begin to help N. and L. They assist with pumping and filling water. Someone brings in a large vessel of milk – the cows have just been milked. A group of boys helps N. start the kitchen fire, with bits of wood and palm fronds. L. is busy washing pots and pans. When the wood stove has been lit, she sets a huge vessel of water on the stove to boil.

The first thing to be made in the morning is *chai*. N. drops tea leaves, cardamom and a large scoop of sugar into a pot of boiling water.

She stirs in some fresh milk – straight from the cow – and boils the mixture up. N. pours out the tea into a large thermos and hands it to a girl standing nearby. She takes it outside and soon several older girls, already dressed and ready for the day, are sipping chai.

This is how the morning starts at the Rainbow kitchen, quietly. But from then on, until about four in the afternoon, N. and L. work non-stop, without any rest. It's as if they're on a roller-coaster for the next nine hours, and can't get off. After chai, they get on to breakfast, and then lunch, and then a snack and by then it is time for dinner. They cook for over hundred people, students and teachers. In the middle of all this, they have to attend in other ways to many people: the woman who milks the cow, an old couple who eat at school and of course the students. One boy whose arm is in a plaster cast hangs around the kitchen the whole day, along with me. Older girls come and go, curious to chat with me, since I am from another country.

While N. cooks, L. doesn't go near the fire at all, if she can help it. She sits against the wall, cutting and slicing vegetables on an *arivalmannai*, the old-style cutting tool. She does have her work cut out – hardly has N. finished cooking breakfast, before L. needs to start preparations for lunch, and more vegetables need to be chopped. N.'s work is really hard. She makes *sambar* in an enormous wide-mouthed pot, and almost simultaneously, boils rice in another huge pot. When the rice is done, she carries the heavy vessel over to the sink, and drains the water out while being bathed in steam.

tamarind

dried red chilli
(round)

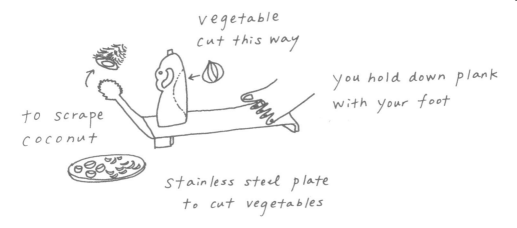

vegetable
cut this way

to scrape
coconut

you hold down plank
with your foot

Stainless steel plate
to cut vegetables

Lunchtime: the three-year olds from kindergarten are the first group to arrive at the dining space. They line up at the counter, each holding out his or her own big stainless plate. A dog hangs around, waiting to pick up bits of food that fall from the children's plates or even out of their mouths. A boy sits on the window sill, leaning on a column. 'He's got the best spot to sit and eat lunch,' I think to myself. I now regret that I smilingly refused the offer of rice from his plate. The boy with his arm in plaster is already eating, ahead of his classmates. A teacher is feeding him, mixing rice and sambar with her fingers and making little food balls that she puts into his mouth. I'm moved by their closeness. This isn't something that exists in Japan today.

An older student comes in and rings a bell in the dining space. Lunch time for older children! Kids rush in … and I eat with this lot too. I end up eating several meals in the school kitchen, with a hundred and twenty people.

At 4.00 pm, N. closes the pot of vegetable rice she has just cooked for dinner. She picks up a few embers from the stove and places it on the lid, to keep the food warm. She then goes over to help L., who is busy scrubbing pots. That done, N. douses the kitchen floor with water and sweeps it out with a broom. It's the end of another day.

The next day, I watch N. and L. cook through the day: *pongal* and coconut chutney for breakfast; rice, sambar, *rasam*, and cabbage for lunch; *puttu* for snack time; and vegetable rice for dinner. Each time for over a hundred people.

When it is time for me to leave, N. is moved to speak. 'We have lots of guests in Vanavil, but you're the first person to visit our kitchen, Nao!' I am very proud to have had that honour. I've noticed how, in spite of her workload, she always adds her own special little twist to each dish, to make it tastier. I find this very moving and generous – especially because the children are so poor, and the school has such a hard time getting quality supplies for the kitchen. I realise that she cooks as if she would for her family and this is her extended family.

As for the kitchen itself, I must admit that when I first saw it, I was startled. It looked like a shack – and one wall was made up of wire netting. But I quickly understood why, as soon as N. lit her wood stove. The wire mesh let all the smoke and steam through, outside and into the fields. During the mornings, I noticed how the atmosphere of the place changed after the stove was lit to make chai. Smoke and steam, along with the smell of chai, softened the place and made us all feel comfortable. The Rainbow Kitchen, I know now, is not merely a 'shack' – it is the centre of the place itself. People gather there to get warm, in different ways. When I opened my sketchbook after I returned to Chennai, I smelt the strong fragrance of kitchen smoke on the pages, and breathed it in deeply.

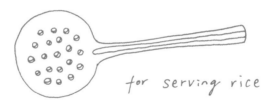

for serving rice

white
tiles

egg case

water from pump
for cooking.

N.'s Ragi Puttu
Steamed sweet millet flour

Originally for 120 people,
modified for 4

500 gms. finger-millet flour
   (ragi flour)
1 tsp. ground cardamon
4 tbsp. sugar
1/2 cup grated coconut

Mix finger-millet flour and cardamom with some warm
water – don't let the mixture get runny, it has to remain dry
and crumbly. Place the dough in a steamer lined with cloth,
and steam for 10 mins. Mix the coconut with sugar and mix
it in to the puttu before serving. You can use jaggery instead
of sugar.

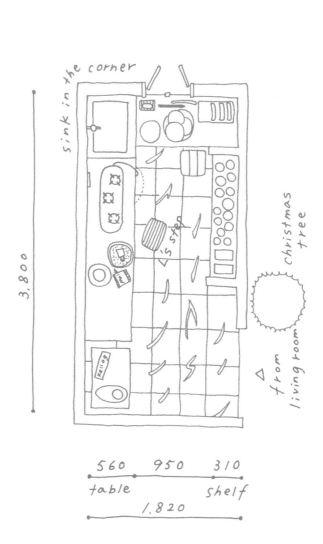

sink in the corner

3,800

5 step

christmas
tree

from
living room

560   950   310

table   shelf

1,820

turquoise
blue for S.

purple for N.

N and S's new dresses
for christmas mass

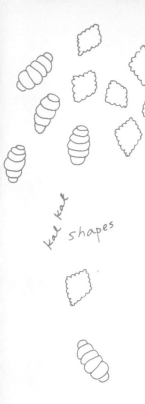

kat kat shapes

ONE WEEKEND BEFORE CHRISTMAS, I'm invited to N.'s home, to be part of their festive food preparations. I have got on well with her from the time I came to Chennai. N. works as an assistant in the publishing house, in charge of many things, and is always busy. She is much younger than I am but much more confident. I love talking to her – as she sits at her office counter I ask her many questions about all kinds of matters, large and small.

N.'s apartment is on the edge of town, where you can still see open fields. We go down a long stretch of road, and then turn into an unpaved street that runs between houses. She and her family have moved into this neighbourhood not too long ago. The building's newly painted blue exterior shines nice and bright. The building has three floors with two apartments on each floor.

N. lives with her mother, L., her sister S. and their dog, Shadow. I don't understand why they have named this cheerful male dog 'Shadow'. They treat him as they would a younger brother. Shadow jumps up and down, and is all over me. 'He gets excited when he sees new people,' I'm told.

The three women lead him away gently into one of the inner rooms. The apartment has two bedrooms, a living room and a kitchen. The view from the living room is open and inviting. There is a wooden cabinet mounted on one wall. I see many pictures of Jesus displayed in it.

L. and N. look similar, especially their feet. L. is the one who cooks. 'I make Christmas sweets because N. and S. ask me to, every year. But I don't make too many different things. I grew up in a large family, and each of us learned to make just one sweet properly. In the end, of course, we had a whole series of sweets for Christmas!'

Her kitchen is new and modern. One wall has a large built-in shelf stacked with supplies and kitchen tools. The working table is L-shaped, with a sink tucked away in the extreme corner. 'How do you use this sink?' I ask.

step to reach
working table

'Indian kitchens are not concerned with practicalities,' they laugh. Since she can't reach it easily, I see that L. has placed a tub of water for use near the sink!

The sweet she's going to make today is called *kal kal*. A cute name, I find. L. puts a scoop of fat to warm in a pan. Meanwhile she mixes wheat flour and powdered sugar in a bowl, and when the fat has heated through, pours it in. I notice that she stands on a small faded blue wooden stool to do this. It looks like a piece of furniture which has been in the family for a while. L. rubs the fat into the mixture until it holds together well. She flavours the dough with rose water and kneads it through.
L. then begins to shape little balls out of the dough, in an interesting way. She presses a ping-pong sized bit of dough on the back of a fork, marking it with grooves. She then rolls it lightly with her fingers, until it looks like a fat macaroni. The dough balls are deep fried in vegetable oil.

I taste a freshly fried kal kal. It tastes good, a simple but distinctive taste – I can't stop eating. L. uses some of the same dough to make diamond shaped pieces that she fries up.

After she finishes making the sweets, L. takes Shadow to the rooftop for some air and exercise. N., S. and I sit down for dinner, which is vegetable *pulav*. They tell me that they usually go to midnight mass on Christmas Eve. 'We went shopping last weekend and got new saris to wear for the mass,' N. tells me. She and S. show me their beautiful purple and green clothes, draping them on their shoulders for me to see. I have known N. for some time at work, but only after I visit her that weekend do I realise that she is the one who supports her family.

On Christmas Eve, N. brings the kal kal which L. made for all of us at the office. Thanks to her, I celebrated Christmas in India.

ALL powders
nicely stored
in containers

L.'s Kal Kal
Fried Sweets

For 6 people

1 kg plain flour
200 gms. fat (butter or ghee)
250 gms. powdered sugar
salt to taste
rose water (or vanilla essence)

Melt the fat in a pan. Mix flour, salt and powdered sugar in a bowl. Add the melted fat, mix thoroughly until the dough holds. Add some rose water and knead through. Shape into ping-pong sized balls. Press each piece against the back of a fork to make grooves, then roll and flatten it until it resembles macaroni. Deep fry the pieces. Alternatively, you can also cut up the dough into little diamond-shaped wedges and fry them.

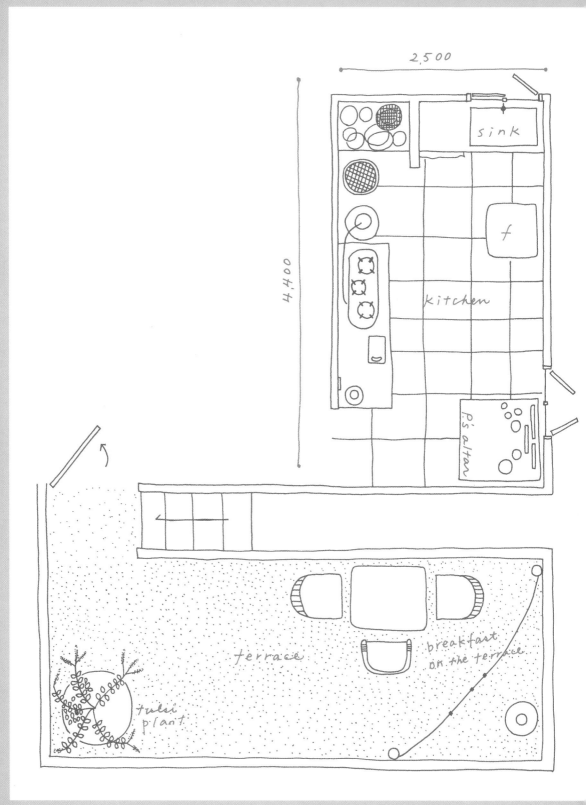

2,500

4,400

sink

t

kitchen

p's altar

terrace

breakfast on the terrace

tulsi plant

CHRISTMAS MORNING

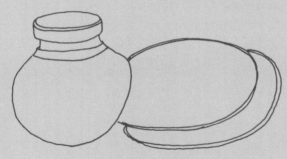

all stainless steel

K. warms
the bottom of South Indian
coffee filter on the stove
to enable a smooth drip

M M

FIRE

THE WEEKEND BEFORE CHRISTMAS, I made new friends. P. and
A. had come to the bookstore in our publishing house, and we got
talking. They said they lived on the next street. 'Come over to our
place for breakfast!' they offered spontaneously. 'How about on
Christmas Day, it's a holiday for us!' I agreed immediately, happy
to have a plan for Christmas morning.

At 7.30 am on December 25, I step out of my apartment, and turn the
corner, to see P. in front of her house. She's looking relaxed and in
her home clothes. It's taken me literally thirty seconds to get to her
place. I'm excited. I haven't done this since elementary school – going
around the corner and dropping in at a friend's place. I go past this
house every day when I go shopping. We open the steel gate, and
climb the staircase to the second floor. We enter a room full of light,
with sunlight streaming in from all directions.

We go into the kitchen, where I see a woman busy cooking. P.
introduces her as K., their cook. She is an older woman, small-made,
and to my eyes looks partly east Asian. I feel warm towards her – she
reminds me of some women in downtown Tokyo. K. does not speak

English, but clearly she understands better than she can speak it. She says something in Tamil, and P. translates for me. 'K.'s really happy that you want to visit her kitchen,' says P.

K. cooks every morning at P.'s house from 7.30 until 9.00 am. She prepares breakfast, makes something to put into the lunch boxes that P. and A. take to work, and gets dinner ready as well. She also cooks for two other families. K. lives with her daughter, and before setting off for work, cooks their food as well. 'My morning starts at 4.30!' says K.

P. and A. have been married for a year. A. is at a university in Chennai. He has a master's degree from the US, and has worked there for five years, before returning to Chennai. P. works in a bank that invests in developing countries. 'When I got married, I tried to cook everyday – but it was too much for me, three meals a day, that's a lot of work.' says P. 'I was wondering what to do, when my cousin introduced K. to me – K. was cooking for her. K. lost her husband when she was thirty-five. Since then she's worked as a cook and managed to raise her two daughters.'

There is an altar on a table in the corner of the kitchen, with a small oil lamp and a *kolam* (a decorative design made with rice powder). P. wakes up early in the morning, prays at the altar, then goes for a jog. She shops for vegetables on her way back. It's her job to buy all the provisions.

Meanwhile, A. is awake and comes into the kitchen. He's full of praise for K.. 'I was sick last week with a bad throat. K. made me hot milk with turmeric, black pepper and honey – it really helped me get over the cold fast. She's really knowledgeable about such things.'

I can see that K. is a good cook – it's evident in the way she goes about things. She is efficient and confident. We're having the

to hold plates
and ladles

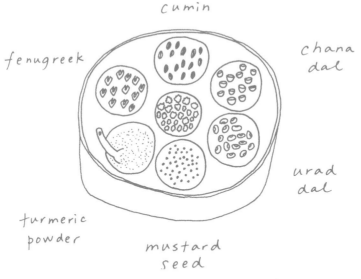

cumin

chana
dal

fenugreek

urad
dal

turmeric
powder

mustard
seed

P.'s spice case
wedding gift from her
mother. (1 year old)

traditional South Indian breakfast of *pongal* (a rice and lentil dish,
a little like firm porridge) with *vadai* (fried lentil patties). K. tells me
that she makes pongal in a pressure cooker with rice and *moong
dal*. 'You need to wait for three whistles on a high flame, then two
whistles on a low flame.' K. talks like a cookbook. 'You cook the
pongal for longer than you would cook rice.' Meanwhile K. gets busy
with spices for tempering it. 'You need a pinch of asafoetida, a bit of
ginger, cashew nuts, cumin, and black pepper fried in some ghee.'
K. tells me. A tasty combination, I can tell even without sampling it.

K. moves on to the vadai. She grinds together soaked *urad dal*,
fresh coriander leaves, mint leaves, black pepper, salt and curry
leaves. The coriander leaves are stored in a stainless steel

container, wrapped in damp cloth. Black pepper comes out of spice box, with little compartments for different spices. 'A wedding gift from my mother,' says P.

Pongal, vadai, chutney, *gotsu* (a relish) and coffee: we end up having an elaborate breakfast. We take our plates out onto the terrace which opens out from their living room. There is a dance school nearby, with a beautifully wooded campus, and sitting here, I can see the trees. Breakfast in the forest, I think.

'It's so nice to have breakfast in this relaxed way.' says A. Maybe this is something special for them as well. We spot two crows sitting on the terrace handrail. 'We think crows are our ancestors, so we feed them,' P. tells me. I ask her what they feed the crows and she says, 'Pongal.' I hope the crows get a less elaborate version.

So we sit there chatting, and begin to make plans to visit their grandfather's farm in Kerala. All too soon, it's time to go. P. and A. have plans for lunch with a friend in the city. I'm going to my friend's place in the evening, to help with cooking for a Christmas party. Meanwhile, I'm filled with gratitude that Christmas morning in a foreign country started the way it did—putting all of us in a very good mood.

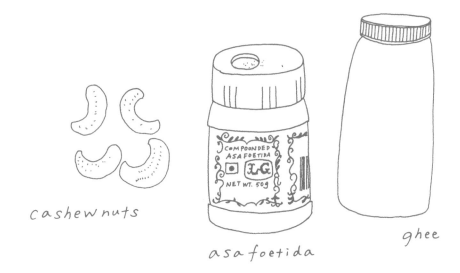

cashew nuts

asafoetida

ghee

K.'s Vadai
Fried Lentil Patties

For 3 people

1 cup of urad dal
fresh coriander leaves
fresh mint leaves
10 black pepper whole spice
salt to taste
curry leaves

Soak urad dal in water for about three hours. Drain off the
water, and grind it in an electric blender into a coarse thick
paste, with the coriander, mint, black pepper, and salt.
Fry curry leaves in oil and add. The mixture should hold
together. Heat oil in a deep pan until it's smoking hot.
Turn down the heat to medium. Take a small piece of vadai
dough and flatten it out. Lay it on a plate. Make a few more,
then fry the vadais in batches until they are golden brown.
Remove with a slotted spoon and place on paper plates,
to drain off any excess oil.

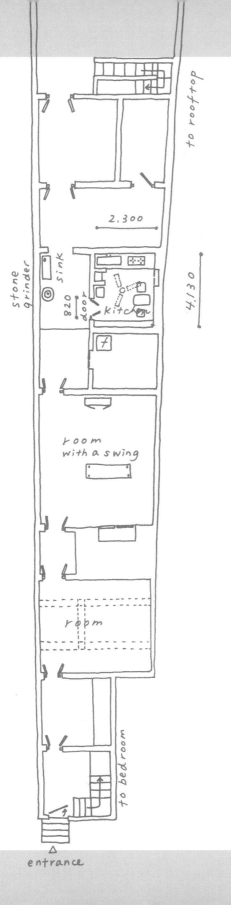

to rooftop

2.300

stone
grinder

sink

820

door

kitchen

4.130

room
with a swing

room

to bedroom

entrance

KITCHEN OF MEMORIES

I ENCOUNTERED R.'S KITCHEN IN AN UNEXPECTED SORT OF WAY.
R. is an astronomer, teaching at the University of Hawaii. He's the cousin of a friend of mine, G., who lives in Chennai. R. was on a visit to his ancestral house in the town of Srirangam, along with his wife, daughter and mother. He was restoring his old family home, where his grandparents used to live. G. said that she was going to drive to Srirangam to see her favourite cousin, and invited me to join her.

The drive from Chennai to the ancient temple town of Srirangam takes about five hours, and we arrive in the evening. R. greets us on the street outside his home, a narrow row-type house which is attached to the neighbouring houses. The scene reminds me of Machiya, an area with old Japanese houses in Kyoto, another historic temple town. R. is busy with the renovation. Women carrying baskets of debris on their heads come out of his house – they are construction workers. I often see women working at construction sites in Chennai too, but they mainly seem to be assistants, carrying materials or cleaning the place. Men on the other hand appear to be doing the actual building.

We stay in a guest house for pilgrims. Life in Srirangam revolves around the huge temple, both for the residents as well as visitors. In this town, the day starts very early. A family staying in the room next to mine wakes at dawn, bustling around and getting ready to go to the temple. For some reason, people knock repeatedly on my door as well. I finally decide to give up staying in bed. It is 6.00 am.

The next knock is R. 'I thought I'd show you around the place, Nao,' he offers. It's a beautiful morning as we set out.

The street is empty and I notice the colourful facades of the row of houses. There is a *kolam* in front of every home, some in white and some coloured, probably because it's New Year's eve.

Kolam is drawn
with rice powder.

A couple of old men sit idly on a bench in front of a house. Nearby, young priests hurry in and out of the temple school. As we pass his house being restored, R. pauses and says, 'My grandparents used to live here. We used to come here almost every summer when they were alive. But I really didn't enjoy it at that time. The town's been cleaned up now, but back then, there was an open drain running behind the house and summers were unbearably hot.'

All the streets in Srirangam are built around the temple complex, in a concentric grid. There are four inner gateways which lead directly to the temple – facing all four directions – and the roads form a network around the gateways. There are houses on every street, starting from the ones closest to the gateways, to the ones on the outer periphery. R.'s house is on an inner road, right next to the temple. By the time I reach the fourth or fifth peripheral road, I notice a dramatic change: the homes on these roads are different. They're not concrete buildings, like the houses near the temple, but thatched huts made of palm fronds. The area around looks barren. It's another world. Later on, I get to know that 'upper' caste people live close to the temple and that the 'lower' caste people live in the outer circles. A typical upper caste house in Srirangam extends from one road to the next concentric one. The facades are narrow, but the houses are long, so the front door opens onto one street, and the back into another.

old swing

Meanwhile, as we stroll back to R.'s place, it's 9.00 am, and workers are busy at the site. We go into the house. The light – so bright and strong outside – immediately becomes muted. As I walk down the length of the house, I notice that it gets steadily darker. But the ceiling is high and there are slits and openings up above, so light still filters in nicely. I walk through alcoves that alternate with large rooms – these alcoves are low-ceilinged, in contrast to the rooms. As I go further in, I experience a steady growing and shrinking of space. After passing through a series of rooms and alcoves, we come to the kitchen, and walk beyond it.

ceiling
fan

We follow the length of the house until we get to an open courtyard, which has a door opening onto a back street. The courtyard has a stairway leading up to a flat roof. We climb up to a fine view across the other rooftops, and I see the white East Gate of the temple. There are workers on the roof, chatting away as they hack at a tree that has rooted in the cracks between two walls. We climb down and make our way back to the kitchen.

The thick wooden door is shut, fitted with a lock. R. unlocks the door and I see a small table and two folding chairs. It makes the kitchen look cosy. There is a sink on the wall to our left, and in front of us, a gas stove on a built in platform. The stove is covered with a cloth. It looks as though the owner of the house left without knowing if she would ever come back. We breathe in air that has been trapped in that room for the past six years. I see dust particles filtered through the light that comes in through a skylight.

The kitchen is rather small but the ceiling is sloping, very high on the left side of the room, and tapering down to the right. I feel as if I'm looking up from the bottom of a milk carton. I take a photograph. The lens is flooded with light, in a way my eye is not – so when I look at my picture later on, the image looks brightly coloured on my computer screen. The faded green of the kitchen walls appears a bright turquoise blue.

There is a fine wooden fan on the ceiling, clearly newer than some of other objects in the kitchen. 'My mother got this fan as a prize for her translation of a Sanskrit poem. So she's very attached to it, proud that it got here through her own efforts. She tells me the story of this fan from time to time,' says R.

R.'s grandparents moved into this house thirty years ago, from another place close by. His grandfather passed away about fifteen years later, and that was when R.'s parents moved in here, to be with his grandmother. They used to live in Mumbai, where R.'s mother worked in a college, teaching English. She retired earlier than she had originally planned, to move to Srirangam.

'When she was teaching, my mother used to wake up at 4.00 am to complete all the household chores, before she left for work.' R. reminisces. 'After she moved here, she continued with the habit, even though she didn't have to leave home. I was studying in the US at the time. When I came home for the holidays, I'd wake up early, jet-lagged, and only my mother would be up at that hour. And she'd already be busy in the kitchen. I would sit here in this chair, and my mother would make *chai* for me. We used to talk a lot in the kitchen.'

After his grandmother passed away some years ago, R.'s parents moved back to Mumbai and no one has been living in this house ever since. R. says he wants to move here, once he retires from his present job in Hawaii.

'Why did you choose Hawaii for your research?' I ask R. 'Because it has the clearest sky in the world,' says R. He's a very kind and patient person—and has spent a lot of time telling me about the town, the temple and his family. But for me, his memories of early morning chai at 4.00 am stand out vividly. That is clearly my favourite story.

4.00 am: a time when the town is still asleep, a time between night and morning, and probably the coolest part of the day to come. Sitting, talking and drinking chai at that hour in this space that seems like the bottom of a milk carton—that must have felt so safe and comforting. This is a kitchen full of memories. It doesn't function anymore, but it still had the power to bring him to this old small town, all the way from Hawaii.

tea table

R.'s Mother's Chai
Indian Tea

For 2 people

2 teaspoon loose leaf tea
2 cup water
4 teaspoons sugar
a few cardamom pods
1/ 2 cup milk

Put all the ingredients into a pot and bring to a boil. Allow it to boil for a minute. Switch off the stove and cover the pot for another minute or two to let the tea brew. Strain the tea into stainless steel tumblers.

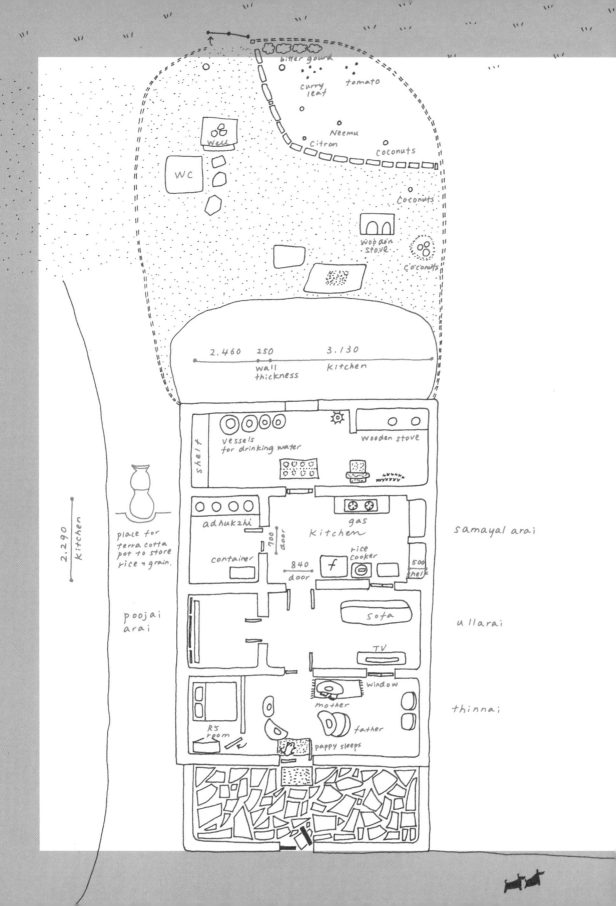

bitter gourd

curry leaf

tomato

Neemu

Citron

Coconuts

Well

WC

Coconuts

wooden stove

Coconuts

2.460   250   3.130
wall
thickness   kitchen

shelf

vessels
for drinking water

wooden stove

2.290
kitchen

place for
terra cotta
pot to store
rice & grain.

adhukzhi

700
door

gas
kitchen

samayal arai

container

840
door

rice
cooker

500
shelf

poojai
arai

sofa

u llarai

TV

window

mother

thinnai

father

R5
room

pappy sleeps

POWER CUT

KITCHEN

New
NGO houses
built in
2006

good
access

farmers

Velankanni
city part

No ships stop by creek

new
part

fishermen's
village

1 km

sea wall was built
after tsunami

Bay of Bengal

Velankanni was hit
by tsunami on the
morning of Dec 26, 2004.

Bay of Bengal

sea wall was built after tsunami

THE JOURNEY TO THIS KITCHEN BEGAN SERENDIPITOUSLY.
I was introduced to an anthropologist who was working with a group
of architects. We got to talking, and when I mentioned my kitchen
project to her, she invited me to a town called Velankanni, where her
team of architects was currently working. That's how I met K. and
from the moment we met, we knew we would be good friends.

Velankanni lies south-east of Chennai, eight hours away by train.
It's a coastal town, surrounded by fishing villages. These villages
were destroyed by the 2004 tsunami, and international aid
organisations built new homes for victims, further inland, away
from the sea. Ten years later, the architects I met were assessing
the life situation of these disaster victims from an architectural point
of view. Some of the villagers have rebuilt or renovated the houses
given to them, to suit their own way of living; others have moved to
new homes to be closer to their kin; and some have moved back to
their old village, willing to take on the risk of living close to the sea.

R. is a woman from the fishing community whose family has moved
back to the coastal village. She's been introduced to me by my new
friends, and I feel very comfortable with her right away. R.'s husband
works in Chennai, and she lives in the village with her small son
and her husband's parents. They open their everyday life to me in
a way that is very special—of course, it's based on the trust that my
architect friends have built up over time.

When I visit them, R. is not yet at home, but her parents-in-law are in.
I'm accompanied by S., an architecture student, who is my translator.
No one in the house speaks English. I'm shown into a small space
where guests are received. Light comes in through the open door,
but beyond the room is darkness.

'This house used to be in the centre of the village,' R.'s father-in-law starts to talk about the tsunami in a hushed voice. He's at home this morning because the sea is stormy, so he hasn't gone fishing. I'm silent as he speaks, and he continues to talk, while showing me wedding pictures of his son and R. 'To escape the waves, I climbed onto the roof of our house, holding my wife's hand. Wave after wave hit us, and went over us. Finally, after several hours, we came down and walked to the shelter.' They were to discover, later, that half their village had disappeared. There was nothing left between their home and the sea. It was not in the centre of the village anymore.

I find the house quite beautiful. I first saw its roof clearly outlined against a broad sky. It's strange to think the tsunami made this lovely sight possible. I stay silent, thinking about all that happened here that fateful year.

'Sorry, you came in earlier than I thought you would.' I look up to see R. come into the house. She's just dropped her son off at kindergarten. Her presence changes the atmosphere in that house and everything is livelier. We follow her to the kitchen. The space where we've been sitting leads into a living room with a sofa and a TV set. It's also a *puja* (prayer) room. The kitchen lies beyond—it's shadowy, lit only by faint sunlight streaming in through the back door. It's a cloudy day. I think that R.'s kitchen is one of the most faraway places I have travelled to.

R. opens a small door to show us the storage room. Large terracotta pots are lined up against a wall. 'We store rice in these pots now. They were used for storing water earlier.' I see a large plastic cool box by the door—a container for fish, perhaps? 'Relief goods arrived in this box. I use it now to store my clothes.' R explains.

She takes a couple of brass lamps from a shelf, fills them with oil, tweaks the cotton wicks and lights them. One lamp goes on the shelf and the other one next to the stove. It is 11.00 am and there is no electricity – they call it a 'power-cut' here. Electricity is cut off every day for two hours in Chennai and up to ten hours in the countryside.

'We started cooking indoors on a gas stove only after the tsunami.' R. says. Once she starts her work, I'm amazed at the speed with which she does things. She scoops rice into a container, hurries out to clean it, returns, puts it on to boil, and begins to take vegetables out of the fridge. 'No fish today,' she says in passing. 'We didn't go fishing because of the storm. So just *pulli kulambu* (tamarind stew) for lunch. Not so interesting for you I'm afraid!'

She seems not to mind the general darkness and moves about quickly. I'm beginning to wonder whether she lit the lamps for my sake, or if she really needs that light. She sits on the floor, and starts to cut eggplants, gourds, beans, radishes and tomatoes expertly, with an *arivalmannai*. Then she grates coconut and grinds it into a rough paste on an old fashioned stone grinder. 'I'd use an electric blender normally, but that's not possible with a power-cut.' she explains.

I see a wooden stove behind her. 'We use the wood stove when gas runs out' says R., and walks outdoors. It's now raining heavily, but she manages to pump water into a large tub, and begins to wash some pots, squatting under the eaves of the roof.

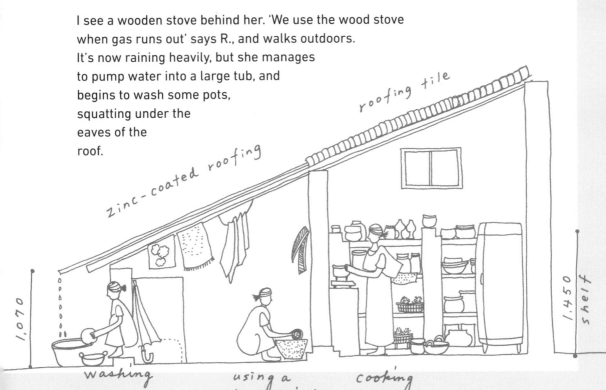

roofing tile

zinc-coated roofing

1,070

1,450
shelf

washing

using a stone grinder

cooking

Raindrops splatter off the roof and the water runs alongside, but she's unperturbed. Her movements are swift, and she uses her long limbs effortlessly.

Meanwhile, in the kitchen, the tamarind stew is almost ready, but R. is not around. We wait. She returns in a bit, with two eggs in her hand – she seems to have gone out to buy them from the nearby kiosk. She cracks open the eggs into a bowl, adds a chopped onion to the white and yellow mixture, and gives it a stir with her fingers. I hear oil spluttering in a pan, into which she tosses the eggs. I've never seen a cook make an omelet in this fashion before. She then opens a small container and takes out some marinated cauliflowers, which look very red. 'Leftovers from my son's lunch box. His favourite.' She deep fries the cauliflower. Time passes quickly in her kitchen.

R. has taken exactly an hour to finish cooking all this: rice, tamarind stew, omelet, and fried cauliflower. S. and I eat lunch right away. R.'s parents-in-law usually don't eat until 1.00 pm. I now understand why R. thought I'd come in earlier than she expected. She normally starts lunch later.

After eating, I stay in the kitchen, sketching. R. goes out and returns in a while, looking very fresh. 'One of our relatives in the village has warm water, so I took a bath at their place.' I notice that her face looks slightly yellow. S. tells me that women in the countryside use

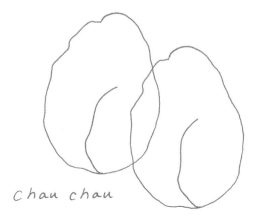

chau chau

turmeric powder on their faces – it's considered good for the skin and makes a person look beautiful. I ask if I can take
a photo of R. 'Sure,' she says. She didn't want her picture taken earlier, when she was cooking. She's agreed now, because she's bathed and ready for a portrait photograph.

The image I have of R. is that of a very strong and bright person. She seemed lit up, surrounded by the quietness in her house. I don't know if this was the result of the rain that left pools of water around her home; or whether the very atmosphere of that old house, its thick walls, breathed a certain quietness.

I think that the power-cut had something to do with it. It played with the sense of space that day. It also marked out a border between times past and present: in the way that R. worked both inside and outside the kitchen, using traditional as well as modern tools.

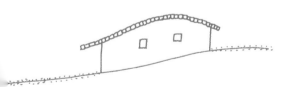

R.'s Pulli Kulambu
Tamarind Stew

For 4 people

2 small eggplants
1 small green gourd (chau chau)
a handful of green beans
2 green chillies
1 white radish
2 tomatoes
lg onion
a pod or two of garlic
A lemon-sized ball of tamarind
1/2 coconut
A sprig of curry leaves
2 tsp. sambar powder
    (spice mix, available in South
    Indian grocery stores)
salt to taste
1 tbsp. oil

Soak tamarind in water and squeeze out the pulp till you have a bowl of thick tamarind juice. Chop the eggplants, gourd, beans, radish and tomatoes. Slice the onion and green chillies. Grate the coconut and grind it with a bit of water – in a blender if you have one. Heat oil in a pan, add onion, garlic and curry leaves. When they are nicely browned, add the vegetables. Now pour the tamarind juice into the pan, add coconut paste, sambar powder and salt to taste. Bring to a boil, then simmer until the vegetables are cooked through.

washing place

N
W E
S

3,470

coconut leaves

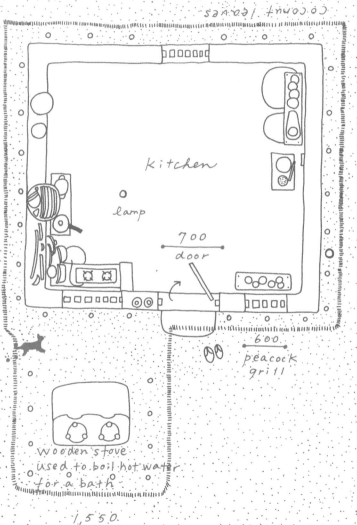

kitchen

lamp

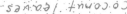
700
door

600
peacock grill

Wooden stove used to boil hot water for a bath

1,550

plaited roof made with dry coconut leaves.
roofing done once a year

Well

230 wall thickness

3,000

2,100

A FAMILY

KITCHEN

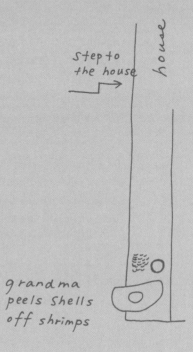

step to
the house →

house

grandma
peels shells
off shrimps

all woven

MY SECOND KITCHEN VISIT IN VELANKANNI also happens through my architect friend K. Late one evening, we visit a tsunami-affected neighbourhood, where architecture students are doing some work with the fishing community. K. is taking me to see a family that has helped them greatly with their research, allowing visiting students to survey their home, and offering a lot of information. It appears that the man of the house has a passion for the history and customs of his village.

As we enter through the gate, we see a group of students surveying the house. BM., the householder, is there with his wife and an elderly woman, clearly his mother. A three-year old is playing nearby, and a tiny newborn baby is fast asleep in a hammock made of the softest sari I have ever seen. The hammock is strung from the rafters of the roof, which slopes down steeply.

Only when I'm inside the house do I understand why the roof hangs so low – it creates a space under the eaves, which is both inside and outside. BM.'s mother sits under it, at the entrance, chatting with her neighbours. We explain to her about my kitchen project, and she immediately invites me to come over for lunch the next day.

As we leave, I catch sight of a mother goat with two baby goats, behind the clothes drying on a line in the yard in the front inner room of the house. A few lights that shine out of the darkness illuminate them in an orange glow. I'm startled at how close they are to human habitation. I think of the time I was walking with K. through the village, and we saw a goat buckle down and fall near a ruined house – it actually died in front of our eyes. Sobered by the thought, I walk silently, until we spot an enormous pig in a field of grass, eating intently. A massive creature that breathes power. We edge past, and come to a house where a woman washes dishes in the yard, surrounded by cackling crows. I'm very still, and tiptoe quietly past the place – I'm really relieved when the crows don't pay any attention to me.

The day after this memorable walk, at 11.00 am, I make my way back to BM.'s place with S., who will interpret for me. Grandma is sitting under the eaves, holding the baby. BM. introduces me formally to his wife, BD. There is a great softness to her. She's just twenty-one. Her mother – like the other women in the village – sells fish. Like other girls, BD. would help her mother around the house, even as a little girl. She did go to school and passed her eleventh grade, but was then married to BM. when she was seventeen. If this was Japan, I'd say that seventeen is too young to be married. But it all looks natural when I look at BD. She lost her twin sister to the tsunami. Everyone I've met in this village has lost someone. The tsunami is part of the everyday conversation here, even though it happened so many years ago. And everyone in Velankanni knows of the tsunami that hit Japan in 2011.

'People in Japan must have had a terrible time, just like us!'
says Grandma. 'When it happened to us, we had help from all over the
world. I wish we could help the Japanese people like others helped us.'

I'm inexpressibly moved by her words. I don't know what to say,
I'm full of respect for this elderly lady who possess so little, yet has
such a generous spirit.

The talk turns to other things, revolving mostly around the family's
three-year old, who has begun to get around a lot. The child has
a mass of curly hair knotted on top of his head. They tell me that
the custom is to let a small child's hair grow out and then shave it
off at some point, offering the hair to god. They have done this once
already with their child, and it will be the second time around soon.

The little boy walks in through the gate into the yard, holding
a small plastic bowl with *appam* (steamed rice noodles) and coconut
milk. Appam is everyone's favourite breakfast food, and he's got his
from a street vendor. We all watch anxiously as he walks unsteadily
towards the house, holding the bowl aloft. He is almost there... when
a crow swoops down to peck at the appam. 'Oooh!' we all cry out.
His father jumps up and flaps the crow away. The child is startled,
but recovers quickly. He sits by his grandma and starts to eat, as if
nothing has happened.

Grandma is busy peeling shrimps. These small shrimps are fresh
and transparent, caught in the local creek. There is a little heap
of sand beside the pile of shrimps. Grandma dips her finger tips
in the sand from time to time – it makes peeling easy.

broad beans

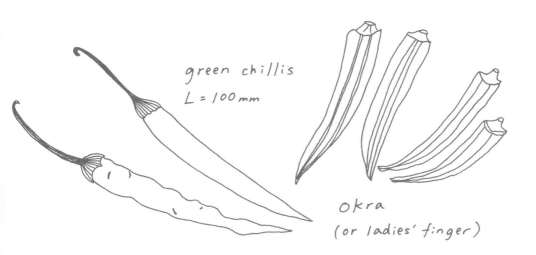

green chillis
L = 100 mm

okra
(or ladies' finger)

Today's lunch is shrimp curry, *poriyal* (sauteed vegetables) and rice. The kitchen is in a separate hut. It is built in the same style as the main house, with an overhanging thatched roof which hangs low and close to the ground. There is a wooden stove under the eaves.

To my surprise, the kitchen is a large space, well organised, the floor cleanly swept. BD. is sitting on the floor, preparing vegetables. Her husband joins her. He is at home today and not out fishing, because of a storm warning at sea. He says that fishing is very hard work, he even goes to sea at night. The family eats what he catches – except on Friday, which is 'vegetarian day'. Many people in Velankanni seem to observe a 'vegetarian day', it appears to be a custom here. 'Do you usually help your wife with the cooking?' I ask. 'Yes, whenever I have time. I love my wife very much.' he says quietly.

green beans

I can tell that he enjoys cooking. He's peeling vegetables expertly with a small knife. BD. meanwhile uses an *arivalmannai* to slice a pile of broad beans. I can see all kinds of vegetables laid out: okra, shallots, carrots, tomatoes, green chillies... I don't know which vegetables go together. The child sits between his mother and father, nibbling a carrot.

BM. speaks some English, and he tells me a little about himself. 'I was born in the village and my father was a fisherman. I'd like my two sons to be fishermen as well.' He knows how to cook because he cooks on the boat. The way he's cutting shallots shows that he knows what he's doing.

As BD. puts the pressure cooker with rice on the fire, BM. slips out and fetches their newborn—it's time for his feed. BD. starts to nurse the baby, and I wonder whether I can take a picture. 'Sorry,' says BM. 'The baby's too small for a photo.' He expresses it nicely, saying that it's also forbidden to photograph a mother who's just given birth or is breast feeding. 'But you can photograph her when she's cooking!' he smiles.

BD. is done with feeding her little one and hands him over. She stands up on tiptoe to check the pot on the stove. 'We have it on a high ledge because we don't want our son to get at the stove,' she explains.

S. and I are asked to eat first. BD. serves us on banana leaves she gets from her neighbours. I'm told that guests are served food on banana leaves. I feel sorry to eat before the family does, but that is how guests are treated here. BD. serves us rice, and then tops it up with shrimp curry. There is also poriyal made of carrots, broad beans and coconut. The shrimp curry is really delicious. The Japanese are sea-oriented people, and to taste of the deep sea is something very special and close to my heart.

broom
secret of the Indian home

After we are done, it's Grandma's turn. She eats from her plate sitting under the eaves, with her grandson next to her. BD. sits down to feed him. She explains that in her natal family, they all ate together, since her father was an open-minded man. In a 'classic' family, she says, people eat one by one, beginning with the head of the family. The women serve all the others and eat last. I have never visited such a family yet. It's very different from Japan, where 'eating together' means we sit around the table and eat at the same time.

Meanwhile a baby goat has wandered in, and Grandma pets him. Apparently a neighbour hit the poor creature because he ate some grain drying outside their house. He hasn't been well since, and is eating nothing. 'I think he's been badly hurt, I'm afraid he may not last too long.' says Grandma sadly. I now understand the manner in which the mother and baby goats are part of the house. They are family.

peacock grill as part of kitchen wall.

BD.'s Shrimp Curry
Tamarind Stew

For 4 people

a heap of small shrimps
2 large onions
a handful of okra
1 tomato
1/2 a coconut
a sprig of curry leaves
a small ball of tamarind
chilli powder to taste
salt to taste
1 tbsp. oil

Peel the shrimps. Soak tamarind in water to extract thin pulp. Grate the coconut. Chop the vegetables and slice the onions. Heat the oil in a pan, add the onions and curry leaves, then the vegetables. Saute for a bit, then add the shrimp and coconut. Tip in the tamarind pulp. Add chilli powder and salt and cook through.

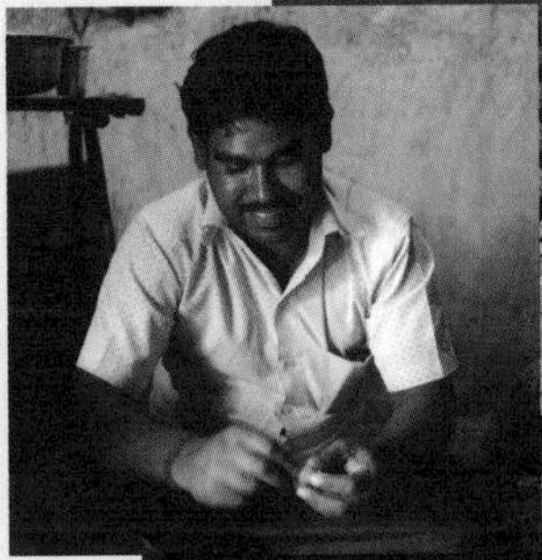

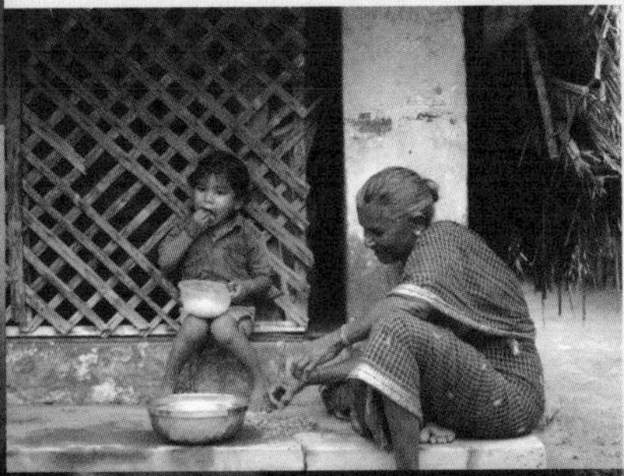

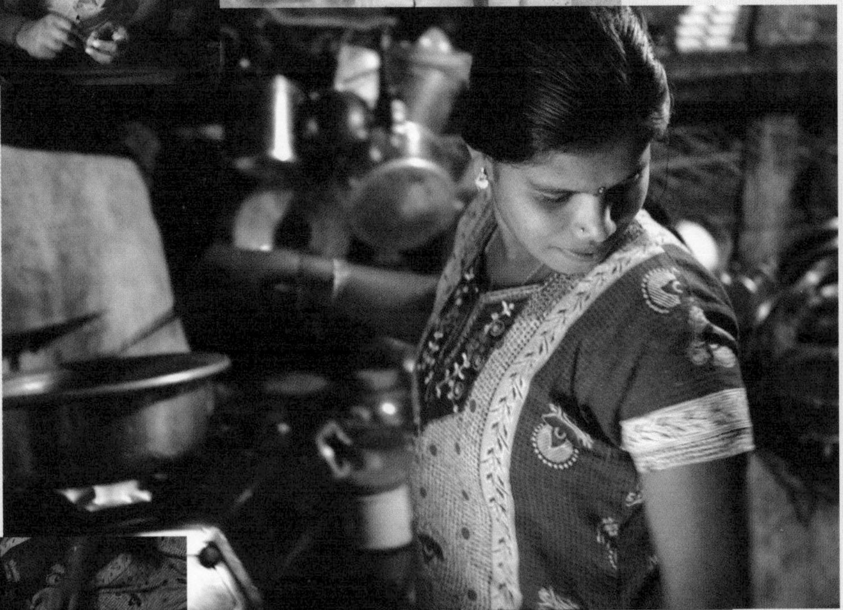

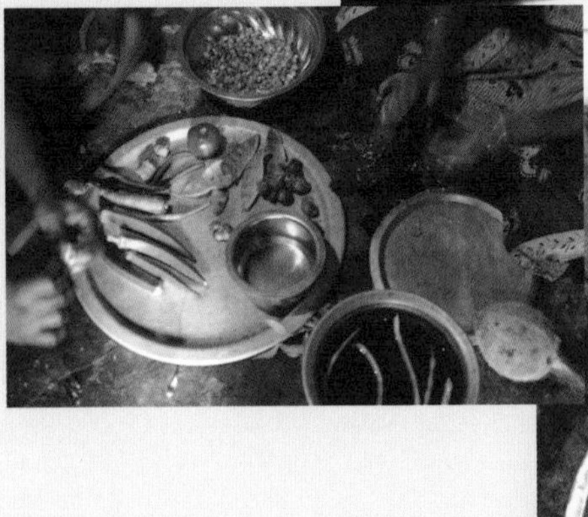

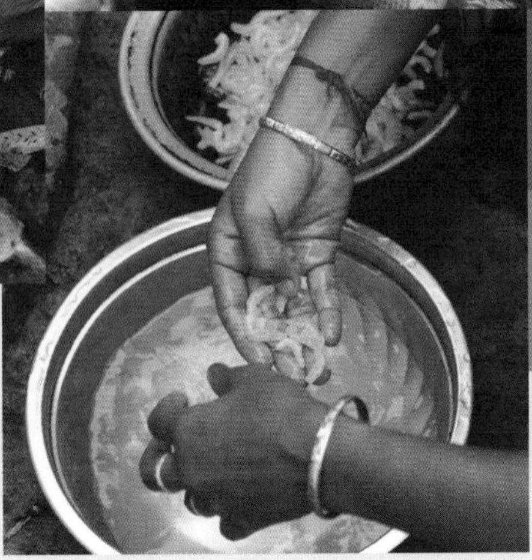

2,900

6100 4900 1200

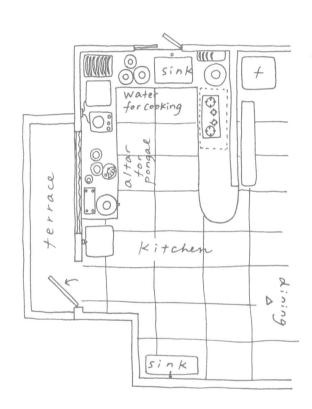

terrace

water for cooking

sink

+

altar for pongal

Kitchen

dining △

sink

kitchen (2F)

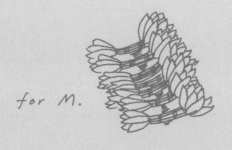

for M.

for N.

cut thread
to divide
into three
parts

for S.

fully bloomed
Jasmine flowers
tied together
with cotton thread

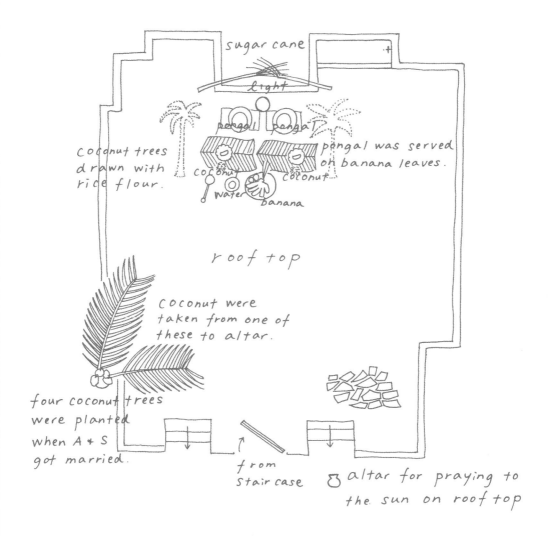

sugar cane

light

coconut trees drawn with rice flour.

pongal pongal

coconut

water

banana

pongal was served on banana leaves.

coconut

roof top

coconut were taken from one of these to altar.

four coconut trees were planted when A + S got married.

from stair case

altar for praying to the sun on roof top

ON A QUIET MORNING IN JANUARY, I get off the bus on the main road of a Chennai suburb. A. is waiting there on his motorbike to take me to his house, which is several streets away. A. is a colleague at work, and heads the production department of the publishing house.

Today is a special day, the start of an important Tamil harvest festival called 'Pongal'. During this three day festival, people offer thanksgiving for the bounties of nature. The sky is blue and clear, reminding me of New Year's day in Tokyo. I'm full of anticipation as we ride through the narrow streets. All the shops are closed, and all the homes have elaborate *kolam*s drawn on their thresholds.

When we reach A.'s house it is only 7.00 am, but everyone is up, bathed and ready, wearing festive clothes. S., A.'s wife, and her mother, R., are busy cooking. S. and I have met before. She heads a nursing college in the city, and is a very caring and competent woman. S. and A. both have full-time jobs. They usually cook together in the kitchen every morning, making both breakfast and lunch for themselves and their two daughters. S.'s mother R. divides her time between S. and her brother.

The kitchen is on the second floor of the building and is open to the dining room. I notice that R. is busy with an altar in a corner of the kitchen, even as she minds the *sambar* cooking on the stove. There are two brass vessels, and a lamp in front of the altar. There's also a plate with betel leaves, turmeric, betel nuts, and assorted fruits. These are offerings to the deity.

'Sorry to make you come so early, Nao. But this year the auspicious time to cook the ritual *pongal* and offer it to god is between 7.30 and 9.00 am.' explains S. 'The time changes from year to year!' I'm curious about the connection between pongal, the rice and lentil dish, and Pongal the festival. I'm told that it is the new rice that is harvested during this season which is used to cook the ritual pongal.

jaggery

$\phi = 110\ mm$

'Today, we cook pongal with new rice that's short-grained and cooks fast,' R. tells me, as she rinses the rice with water. 'We're making two kinds of pongal, sweet and savoury.' She pours the water she has rinsed the rice with into two special vessels near the altar.

S. is busy with a shopping bag, taking out what looks like tender ginger, but with a long stem and leaves.

'Is that ginger?' I ask. 'Yes. We do eat ginger with leaves when it's in season. This is ginger, but that's turmeric. Look, the roots are different.' S. ties the ginger and turmeric to the rim of the vessels which contain the water rinsed from the rice. They look splendid, all dressed up. S. goes on to fill the lamp with oil and light the wick.

'We pray to these vessels that hold the rice water, before we start cooking the ritual pongal.' S. explains. After the prayer, she unties the ginger and turmeric, so that the pots can go on the fire.

R. sits down on the floor with an *arivalmannai* and begins to cut up a large ball of jaggery into little bits and pieces. Meanwhile, the rice water is boiling in both the pots, and S. tips rice and *moong dal* into each of them.

Then she picks up a garland of jasmine flowers from the counter, snips off a length, and tucks it into her hair. 'I'd love to give you flowers, but you have short hair, Nao!' she says. She calls out to her daughters in the living room. They're drying their hair, and watching Doraemon, a Japanese cartoon film. It feels odd for me to hear the familiar character speak in Tamil. S. pins flowers on her daughters' hair, and R. tucks a single yellow flower into her own. Many Indian women have long hair and wear it in a braid,

R. put yellow flowers in her hair. The same flower was placed on turmeric cone on the altar in the kitchen.

often with flowers. I've seen women making jasmine flower garlands in front of temples – people buy them for their hair or to offer at the temple altar. The flowers last a day, and turn into a dried-out dark brown by the late evening. That's why people buy flowers every day. It's a beautiful custom, but what is exotic to me is perhaps not so for the women here.

'I wear flowers in my hair only on special days like Pongal,' says S. I understand. I've also grown up in a country where old customs remain in contemporary life. 'We're making pongal in pots today,' S. goes on. 'But that's because my mother's cooking. I usually make pongal in a pressure cooker, especially when it's an everyday breakfast. It just takes less time. Cooking in the morning doesn't take more than half an hour at our home!'

cardamom

Suddenly I hear the sound of chanting. 'Pongal O Pongal!' calls out R. I hurry over to see what is happening, and find her standing next to a pot of rice and milk, which is boiling over. I'm startled. S. comes in to explain: '"Pongal" in Tamil means that which overflows. Abundance. So we let milk, in which the rice is being cooked, boil over on Pongal day – we're praying for abundance in the harvest season.'

All this has happened so quickly, I've hardly had time to take it all in. I thought pongal was just a rice dish, but it turns out that there is a really deep significance to the word.

When the pongal is ready, we all move to the rooftop. The sun is already strong, and light is streaming down on us. R. starts making another altar, with everybody's help. A. pulls a green coconut off the top of a tree growing close to the terrace and splits it open with a machete. There are four coconut trees surrounding A. and S.'s house, planted when they were married, fifteen years ago. Two of the trees are taller than their house. The altar gets ready, with the two pongal pots placed next to it. It's surrounded by coconuts, sugar cane pieces, flowers and other offerings. R. lays down some banana leaves, puts portions of pongal on them, and tops it with peeled bananas. These are offerings to the sun and sky.

R. lights the lamp and as everyone gathers around, the two children sing traditional Tamil songs. Their singing is very moving, and I know this moment – with those clear melodious voices – will stay with me for a long time.

A woman from next door comes up the stairs, with a baby on her hip, and a plate of pongal in her hand. She offers the pongal to the sun, quickly, and then goes back down the stairs.

'Tamil people usually go home to their villages to celebrate Pongal,' says A. 'Any of our neighbours who hasn't gone always join us for the day. But wherever they are – America, Singapore, Australia – everyone makes pongal on the festival day and offers it to the sun. It can be quite simple. Even we – we're doing everything in the traditional way today only because R. is here. Otherwise we celebrate rather simply.'

Once the ceremonies are over we go downstairs and have breakfast: sweet pongal and savoury pongal. The savoury pongal comes with a special sambar today: drumstick, radish, sweet potato, and green beans.

While we eat the dish which has the same name as the day, I reflect on the word, and all that I've learned today. 'Pongal' actually refers to a moment, the exact instant of boiling over, when something overflows. I'm struck by the sophistication of the Tamil people: they have a name for a moment that can't be known for certain, and they've created a festival around that moment.

brass vessels are used
only during pongal festival.
In country side, people use clay pots.
every year they use new pots for
pongal festival.

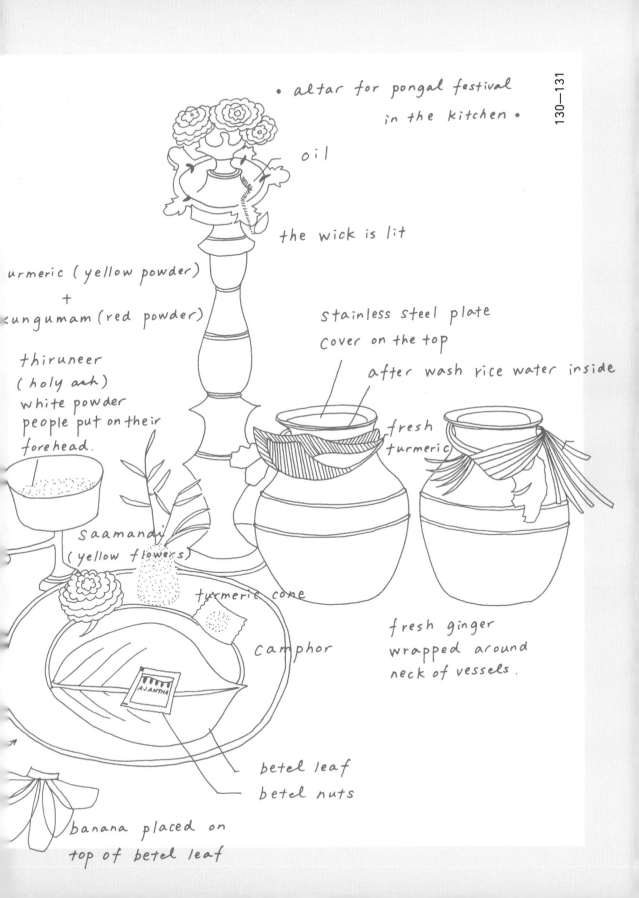

• altar for pongal festival in the kitchen •

oil

the wick is lit

turmeric (yellow powder)
+
kungumam (red powder)

thiruneer
(holy ash)
white powder
people put on their
forehead.

stainless steel plate
cover on the top

after wash rice water inside

fresh
turmeric

Saamandi
(yellow flowers)

turmeric cone

camphor

fresh ginger
wrapped around
neck of vessels.

AJANTHA

betel leaf
betel nuts

banana placed on
top of betel leaf

R.'s Sakkarai Pongal
Sweet Rice and Lentils

For 6 people

2 cups raw rice
1 cup of milk
1 cup moong dal
2 balls of jaggery
    (around 800 gms)
1 grated coconut
1 tsp cardamom powder
a handful of cashew nuts
3 tbsp. ghee

Cook rice and moong dal together in milk and water (you can use a pressure cooker). Heat water in a pan and while still on the stove, break the jaggery balls into it. Stir until the jaggery melts. When cooled, run the melted jaggery through a sieve to get rid of the dregs. Add cardamom powder, the melted and cleaned jaggery and the grated coconut to the cooked rice and dhal. Let the mixture simmer on a low flame until it turns a uniform golden-brown. Turn off the flame. Heat ghee in a small pan and fry cashew nuts lightly. Add to the pongal.

big fan above gas

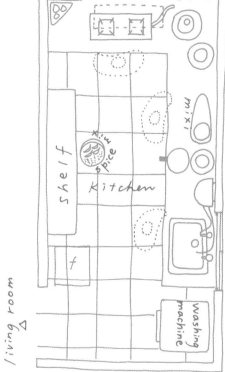

shelf

Kitchen

spice

mixi

f

washing machine

living room

fruits on tiles

A TASTE

O F H O M E

rice

toor dal

turmeric

fenugreek

channa dal

coriander

I ARRIVE AT THE LONG-DISTANCE BUS TERMINUS in the city. It's teeming with people, and I smell sweet bread from the many kiosks around. I'm not leaving Chennai, this is just where I agreed to meet M., a colleague from work who is taking me to visit his family. They live close by. This area is the western part of the city, and has many more large apartment complexes than the south, where I live. M. picks me up punctually at the terminus. He's become a good friend. M. has lived and worked outside India, so he understands people who come from other places.

We arrive at a two-storey apartment, where M.'s in-laws live. M.'s own place is close by, but during the weekend, the extended family spends most of their time here. I think this is quite an ideal way of living in a big city.

The apartment has a living room, a kitchen, and two bedrooms and seems like a large space for two people. M.'s wife P., her mother, B., and her sister-in-law V., are busy cooking. V. is taking the rind off a kind of yam which has been steamed in a pressure cooker. I'm told this vegetable is called *karnakizhangu* in Tamil. We have a similar looking root vegetable in Japan, only smaller in size.

P. is an elementary school teacher. 'I'm busy with school on weekdays, so I make sure I visit my mother over the weekend and spend time with her,' she says. I notice how alike she and her mother are.

P. points to what they're making: 'We're having *puli kulambu* (tamarind stew), *aviyal* (vegetable stew with coconut and yoghurt) and rice today.' They usually cook a meat dish – like chicken curry – on weekends, but they've chosen to cook a vegetarian meal for me.

V. is now getting the rice ready. P. puts the pressure cooker on the stove, then looks to the *sambar*. Her mother is busy getting the ingredients ready for aviyal, to go into the pressure cooker. It's obvious that they're used to cooking together, dividing up the tasks easily between each other, each anticipating what the other needs. I find it beautiful, the slow rhythm of their cooking. It's also nice to see a kitchen in which three women can chat and cook happily together. They clearly enjoy their weekend routine.

P. is adding spices to the puli kulumbu. 'We tip in three spoons of this spice usually, but today let's keep it to two spoons—a less spicy kolambu for Nao.' But I still see a spice mountain on the vegetables frying in a pan for the kulambu.

'Is that spice mix home-made?' I ask.

'Yes,' says P. and brings down a plastic bucket from the shelf to show me the whole spices and *dals* that go into the mixture. 'Many people still make their own spice mixtures at home. Look, these are the ingredients we use. They need to be roasted and ground together. We need around three kilos of spice mixture every six months!' she says. P. then names each of the spices for me, and explains how much of it needs to go into the mixture. 'When you make this mixture, you have to roast each ingredient separately, but they can be ground together.' she adds. 'This is my mother's recipe, which we all follow. I grind my own at home, and so does V. By the way, V. is from Andhra Pradesh, but she's learned a lot of Tamil dishes from my mother.'

V. and her husband have recently relocated to Chennai from the US. 'I cooked Indian food even when we lived in America. You can get all our ingredients there!' says V. There are lots of Indian people living in Tokyo now as well, and as I listen to the three women speaking, I'm beginning to understand how Indians travel. They carry their mothers' recipes with them. If you have your spice mix, you can take your kitchen with you wherever you go. It may not replace the comfort and companionship of cooking with your extended family, but it does have the taste of home.

spice bucket

B.'s Podi
Spice Mix

For a family of 4

200 gms red chilli
200 gms coriander seeds
3 tbsp turmeric whole
    (or powder)
4 tbsp whole cumin
2 tbsp black pepper
2 tbsp mustard seed
2 tbsp methi (fenugreek) seeds
2 tbsp toor dal
2 tbsp channa dal
2 tbsp urad dal
2 tbsp raw rice

Roast all ingredients separately (without any oil) and then grind them together in a blender. Store in an airtight container.

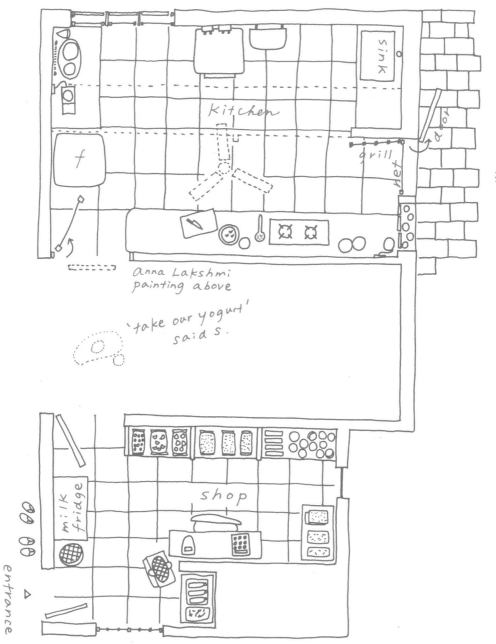

sink

kitchen

grill

net

door

3 kinds of doors

f

Anna Lakshmi painting above

'take our yogurt' said S.

milk fridge

shop

entrance

curry leaf

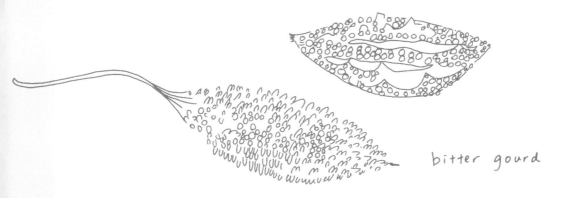

mint +
coriander

EARLY ONE MORNING, I set off to visit a nearby shop that sells organic vegetables. The place – which has been recommended by a friend – is in a quiet residential area close to the beach. There is a small sign outside the gate, and as you go in, there are two doors. One leads into a house, and the other to the shop. Shining potted plants stand in a row on a lawn – they've just been watered. It's going to be another hot day.

I hear women's voices coming from the shop. As I enter, I'm greeted by S., the owner, who's at the cash desk. She's expecting me, since my friend has already told her I would stop in. 'Thanks for coming,' she says, holding my hands in both of hers, and looking at me directly. 'Would you like to stay for breakfast?' She has big, warm hands and looks about my mother's age. She wears a nicely starched cotton sari. My first impression is that she and her husband K. like to welcome people into their home and their shop. This is confirmed by what I get to know of them later.

I look around. The shelves are stocked with all the basic vegetables used in South Indian cooking: tomatoes, green beans, bitter-gourd, drum sticks, eggplants, coconut, raw banana... a basket with a wet linen cloth over it contains fresh mint and coriander leaves. All the produce is grown at their organic farm.

Their kitchen is behind the shop. It is a big independent room and has large windows on all three sides. Annalakshmi, the goddess of grain, graces the door to the kitchen. I'm introduced to P., a helper at

bitter gourd

coconuts

the house who's in charge of cooking. She's making *kuzhi paniyaram* with a simple chutney. She grinds together red chilli, roasted *channa dal*, salt, and a sprinkling of water, tempers it with a bit of seasoning, and chutney is ready. It's the simplest chutney I've ever tasted.

After this initial introduction, I'm a frequent visitor at their place. I learn a great deal about traditional food processing from S. On one of my visits she shows me a package of dried bitter-gourd and explains to me how it is sliced, salted and sun-dried. It keeps for many months, and apparently these kinds of dried vegetable condiments used to be very common in traditional kitchens earlier. On another day, she opens her fridge, spoons out a scoop of her home-made yogurt, puts it in a plastic bag and hands it to me. 'You should make yogurt at home. Just warm some milk, not too warm, and add a spoon of yogurt. Leave it for a couple of hours at room temperature. If you make it at noon, you'll have yogurt in the evening.'

It's a special learning experience for me, to go back and forth from the shop to the kitchen, getting to know South Indian vegetables, and what to make with them. On one occasion S. shows me a bundle of greens: 'We call this *mullai keerai*, they're amaranth leaves.' I know amaranth seeds, but not the fresh leaves. I learn that keerai in Tamil means greens or spinach. There are many kinds of keerai, and several ways of cooking them, but this is one of S.'s favourites: 'Cook together a bit of *moong dal* with chopped keerai, then stir in cumin powder and some grated coconut. Season with some mustard seeds in a bit of hot oil.' I've tried out S.'s recipe many times – it's really tasty each time I make it, and somehow, I've never forgotten that initial taste.

S. and I also have interesting conversations about growing food. 'Do you know Masanobu Fukuoka?' she asks to my surprise one morning. I haven't heard that Japanese name for a long time. 'K. and I were deeply moved by his book 'One-straw Revolution' when we were young. We've wanted to be farmers ever since.'

Though they had wanted to do this for a long time, it was only after their two children grew up did S. and K. take up organic farming. Around ten years ago, they bought land in a village outside Chennai city, and K. quit his job in a large company to concentrate on farming. They invite me to visit their farm.

At 6.00 am one morning, we head out of the city on the highway, into the countryside. After a long drive, we turn off into a village. I notice the decorated horns of the cows in the field. It's just after Pongal, the Tamil harvest festival. The village homes are all thatched, made of palm leaves. Their farm is at the end of the village.

As we come through the gate, I see a banana and coconut plantation. A family of cows is munching in front of a cowshed. There are people already working on the farm, and a woman is busy trimming the lawn. They have a beautifully maintained garden.

K. and S. explain to me that they use cow manure and urine to fertilize the land naturally. They believe in using the traditional

drumstick

panchagavya (five kinds of products from the cow) to keep their land fertile: dung, urine, milk, curd and ghee. They cultivate rice, fruits and vegetables on their farm, and from their cows get their basic dairy products. Basically all the ingredients used in South Indian cooking are available on their farm, including tamarind.

Over the ten years that they have done this, their organic products are doing well. They have also started to work with local farmers, educating them about natural farming. K. stays on the farm during the week, working alongside the other farm workers. S. is in charge of the shop in the city.

'What do you do for your food when you are on the farm?' I ask.

'S. makes lots of *idli*s at the beginning of the week for me to take to the farm. I just warm them up!' says K. I'm astonished that he is content with such a simple meal – such a contrast to all the produce available at their large farm. But then I think that K.'s attitude to what he eats is in keeping with his philosophy of organic farming.

Their kitchen in the city is likewise special. It's not just for themselves, but always has space for others. Just as they have introduced local farmers to natural farming, their kitchen door is open to city people who want to start discovering the farm behind the kitchen.

bunch of
bananas

P.'s Kuzhi Paniyaram
Fried Dumplings

For 4 people

3 cups boiled rice (can be
    substituted with raw rice)
I cup urad dal
salt to taste
oil for frying
kuzhi paniyaram pan

Soak the rice and *urad dal* separately for a few hours, and grind them into an idli batter (details and recipe on p. 190). Let the batter ferment overnight and stir it thoroughly the next day, adding salt to taste. Heat the kuzhi paniyaram pan and dribble some oil into each hollow, making sure they are all greased. When the oil is hot, pour a ladle full of batter into each hollow. As the dumplings cook, dribble a little oil on to each of them. They should fry very gradually, and brown on all sides. To make sure they are evenly browned, roll them about in the pan with the help of a small knife. Remove the dumplings carefully, and start on another batch, until you have enough for four people. Serve with a chutney.

to garden

to washing room

electricity connects from here

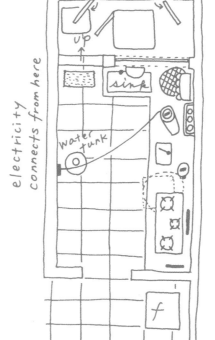

UP

sink

water tank

f

bucket
with
rice

POIL
NATI

a bag of
chilli

iron pan

entrance

A N   I N T E R N A T I O N A L   K I T C H E N

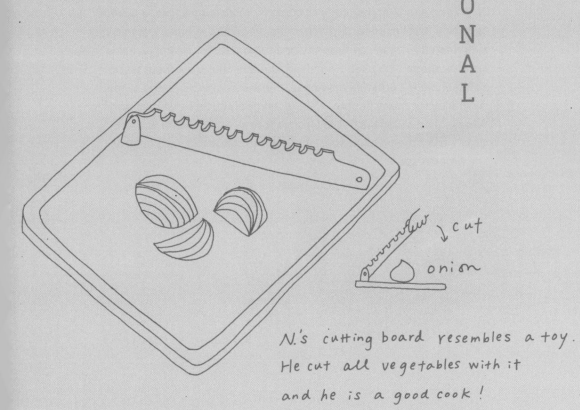

↓ cut

onion

N.'s cutting board resembles a toy.
He cut all vegetables with it
and he is a good cook!

R. AND I ARE ABOUT THE SAME AGE. We became friends when I visited the school she started in Nagapattinam, and now I'm dropping in to the home she shares with her partner N. She's warned me that she lives in a small and dark apartment. But when I arrive, that seems to be far from the case. It's actually quite spacious, an apartment in a building complex that reminds me of houses built during the Showa period in Japan, around the 1970s. I feel nostalgic just looking at it, especially the outer wall of concrete blocks. There's a huge tree outside the gate, and the ground is carpeted with flowers. When I enter their apartment on the first floor, I find that R. and N.'s place is actually bigger than mine in Tokyo.

N. is an artist. He paints and sculpts, and runs a studio with several other young artists. They are often found at his house, and help with cooking. N. and I introduce ourselves to each other. He's shy and quiet. R. is more talkative, and translates his Tamil into English. She informs me that she isn't the cook in their house, he is.

N. is to cook a beef dish today. I come from a country where people love beef, but I'm uncertain about who eats beef in India. I'm told that it is related to caste, community and region. N., for example, grew up in a village with over a hundred families, many of whom were related to each other. In his house, there was always plenty of food available, for many people. 'People eat beef there, as well as pork,' N. says. This village is not far from a forest, and much of N.'s art draws from the primal experiences of his childhood, particularly the time he spent in the forest.

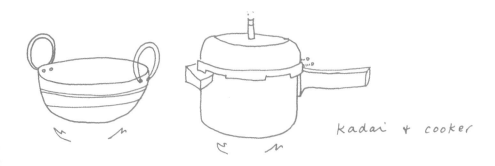

kadai + cooker

fresh coriander
& salt ↘

N and R love the soup
from cooked beef and vegetables.
'mother used to let me have a
soup while she was cooking like this.'
N. said.

R. tells me about a recent solo art exhibition, featuring N.'s work, when a friend of hers presented a poem on the opening evening: 'It's called "Beef, Our Life" and I think it answers many of your questions. Beef is considered Dalit food. Since Dalits are supposed to be "untouchable" and "low", the food they eat is also considered "low". It's the case even today. But lots of young people eat beef these days – especially those who've travelled abroad and tasted steak in other countries. So that makes N. international doesn't it?' R. jokes.

N. gets busy with cooking. His kitchen is narrow, with a window that opens to the outside. There is a working table in a corner, with a bowl of beef on it. I can tell that it's good meat, and N. says it's from a local shop, not far from where I live. 'I buy different cuts and mix them up, the meat tastes better that way,' he says. He puts the meat into a pressure cooker with onion, fresh coriander, curry leaves, and some water and sets it to cook.

The cooker begins to whistle in a while, and the room fills with the fragrance of fresh meat broth. N. opens the cooker and pours out some of the clear liquid into bowls. He adds salt and chopped coriander, and offers me a bowl. 'Some soup?' he asks.

tomato cut this way

'It's not strictly part of traditional Indian cuisine, but we do enjoy broth like this, which comes out of the cooking process. My mother always gave it to me to drink, when I was little.' It's quite delicious, and R. drinks up her bowl with a smile.

N. opens a spice kit and takes out cloves, black pepper and cardamom. 'I always use whole spices,' he says, as he chops up tomatoes and puts them in a blender. He cooks slowly. But it's not a matter of getting it done, as far as he's concerned. He enjoys the moment. He takes time off to smoke, stubs out his cigarette and returns to the stove. 'Let's invite some friends. There's lots of food.' he suggests.

R. starts calling up people. And in a while, when lunch is almost ready, some young men arrive, all smiles. N. has cooked a very luxurious lunch by this time: beef curry, shrimp curry, fried fish, *rasam* and rice. We sit down to eat a hearty meal. The beef curry has a very deep and complex taste. All the food gets eaten up – everyone feels very full and happy.

• spice pack for beef curry •

bay leaf   cinnamon bark

cardamon

nutmeg

poppy seed   black pepper

somph

I read the Beef poem later. It's by a Dalit writer, and in the poem she talks of her community's relationship to the cow. The poem speaks quietly and honestly about a fundamental question: how do we build relationships with domestic animals? It's a question for all of us.
She then links this question to other larger issues.
Here are some lines from the poem:

From Beef, Our Life
by Gogu Shyamala

Beef is our culture,

Beef – our living green nature.
Life's diversity, breath of our soul.
'Don't eat beef!'
'But how?' I ask you.
Another question. Who are you to tell me what to eat?
...
We respect the cow that births the bull.
We feed her fresh grass, tender jowar stalks and rich rare fodder.
We don't make her work,
...We graze her well, so that her calves grow strong,
We nurture the cow with an eye to cultivation.
At times when we are happy and relaxed
In celebration, we gather contributions, go to the fair.
And buy a healthy, strong cow to bring down, cut and share.

(Translated from the Telugu by R. Srivatsan with help from Susie Tharu, N. Manohar and Jayasree Kalathil)

N.'s Maattu Kari
Beef Curry

For 5 people

Various cuts of beef
2 onions
2 tomatoes
two sprigs of curry leaves
a bunch of coriander leaves
1 tbsp. ginger and garlic paste
2 tsp. chili powder
1 bay leaf
a few pieces of whole cinnamon
2–3 clove
1 tsp poppy seed
3 whole cardamom
a pinch of nutmeg
1 tsp whole black pepper
1 tsp fennel seeds
salt to taste
1 tbsp. oil

Slice onions and chop tomatoes. Puree the tomatoes and grind all the spices in a blender. Pressure cook beef, onions, half the curry and coriander leaves, and 2 cups of water in a pressure cooker. Fry sliced onion and curry leaves in a frying pan. Add the cooked beef and onions, tip in the spice-mix, chili powder and fresh tomato puree. Simmer for about 20 minutes. Add salt to taste and the remaining coriander leaves before you take the curry off the stove.

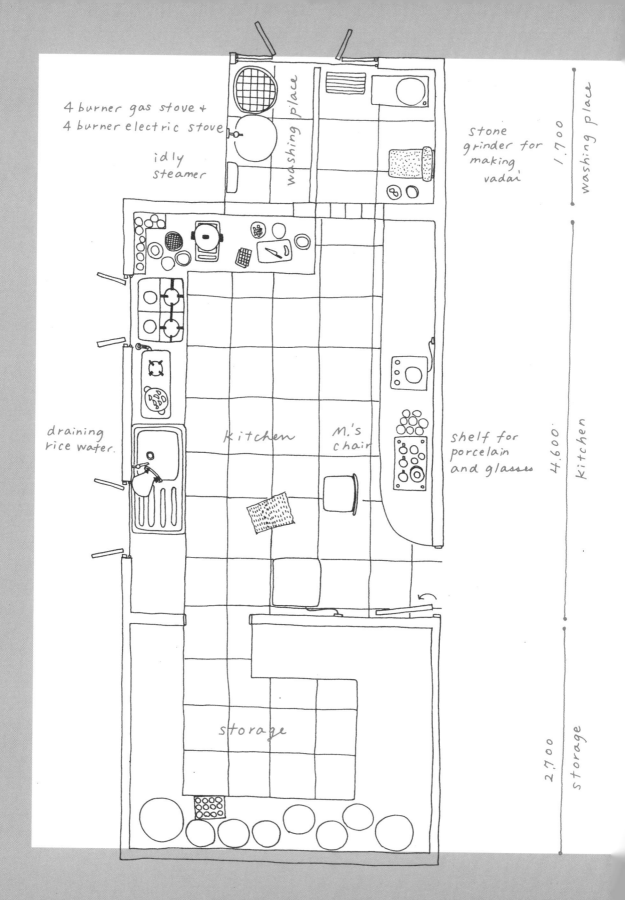

4 burner gas stove +
4 burner electric stove

idly
steamer

washing place

stone
grinder for
making
vadai

1.700

washing place

draining
rice water.

Kitchen

M.'s
chair

shelf for
porcelain
and glasses

4.600

Kitchen

storage

2.700

storage

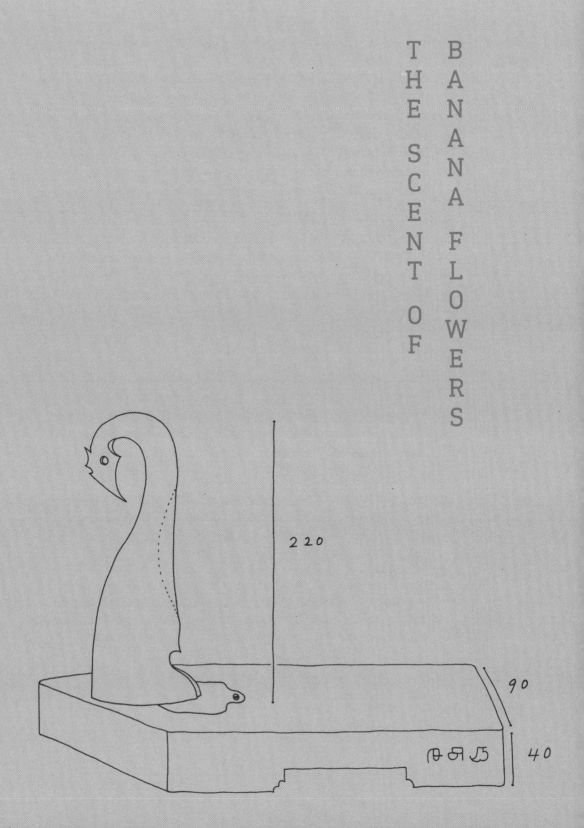

220

90

40

ଙ ୬ ୫

shallots

WHEN I BEGAN MY PROJECT ON SOUTH INDIAN KITCHENS, I was told that there is a very distinct Tamil cuisine called Chettinad. It's also the name of a region, and many of Tamil Nadu's important merchant families come from there. I had once seen a Chettinad-style house in a local museum: it was an opulent structure with massive teak windows and doors, beautiful tiles and antique furniture. It had obviously belonged to upper class people with a unique culture of their own.

Chettinad cuisine – which is an important part of this culture – is famous for its distinctive use of spices. To get to know this, a friend, C., has offered to take me to her mother M.'s house and cook for me there under M.'s guidance. M. is said to be a wonderful cook herself, specialising in traditional Chettinad food. C. and I chat along the way, and from our conversation it's evident that C. is from a family and community who have built their prosperity over a long period of time. The feeling stays with me through the day.

M. lives with her husband, as well as their son and his family. Their home is a large three-storey mansion, housing twelve people. We enter through a room with a very high ceiling. The dining room is to the left, with a large dining table seating at least ten people. I've never seen such a table in any of the homes I have visited.

M. looks to be in her 70's. She moves slowly because of her bad knee, and we follow her to the kitchen. It's a bright south facing space with a high ceiling and plenty of light. I'm introduced to a slender and smiling young man and a small-made woman: G., the cook and A., the house helper.

M. sits in a chair in the middle of the kitchen – it gives her a good overview of all the kitchen activities, from washing vegetables to cooking. This is her usual sitting place, I gather. 'G. came to us around five years ago. For the first six months, I devoted all my time teaching him our cuisine. He's North Indian, from Bihar, and South Indian food was new for him,' M. tells me.

I see that the vegetables are all washed and ready in a sieve. C. gets to work immediately, all the while translating M.'s Tamil into English for me. She starts by cooking rice in a large vessel, and when it's nearly done, clamps a lid on the vessel and turns it upside down. 'You let out the starchy water. That makes the rice fluffier.'

She then gets to work on the eggplant gravy. She slices a large eggplant – it's from their own organic farm in Chettinad. She adds whole shallots to the sliced eggplant, then heats oil in a pan. Whole fennel, fenugreek and mustard seeds go into the hot oil, followed by garlic pods, turmeric, chilli and coriander powder. Once the spice mixture is fried through, C. adds the eggplant and shallots, then pours in some tamarind juice and a cup of cooked *dal*. 'We cook a good quantity of dal in the morning and use it in several dishes,' C. explains.

The special item on today's menu is banana flower *vadai*. The small white-and-yellow banana florets have already been removed from the large flower and cleaned. 'It's the cleaning which takes some time. You need to carefully remove the bitter inner parts of the florets. That's why we finished doing that early this morning,' says C.

A. picks up the ingredients for the vadai and moves to a small adjoining room. There is a stone grinder here, made of a large stone with a hollowed out mortar and a large pestle which fits into the hollow. The room also has a washing space at floor level, used to wash vessels. A. is going to grind soaked dal, banana flowers and some spices in the stone grinder. She begins with the dal and spices, and I'm mesmerised by the heavy rhythmic sound of stone circling on stone, which goes on for quite some time. It must be really hard work, but A. looks impassive throughout.

brinjal (eggplant)

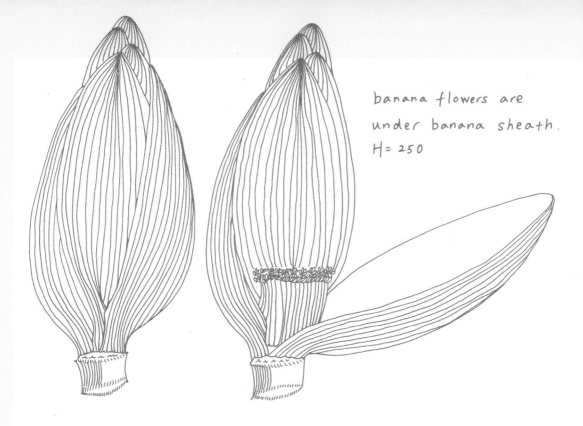

banana flowers are
under banana sheath.
H = 250

After crushing the dals and spices, she starts adding the banana flowers, bit by bit. As they are ground into the mixture, the flowers let out water and turn brown. A. grinds the mixture into a coarse but firm batter. When she's done, she scoops it out of the stone mortar and pestle, making sure to take out every last bit. I always love to see this part of the grinding, the thoroughness with which it is done, so nothing is wasted.

I notice now that ground banana flowers give off a distinctive scent – I haven't smelt anything like this before. It's a very faint fragrance, slightly sweet and very distinct.

'This vadai is my absolute favorite dish,' says C., as she adds coriander leaves, chopped onions and salt to the batter. She makes tiny balls out of this mixture, flattens each one on the palm of her hand, and fries them in oil. C. cooks quickly and G. helps her. I assume this is how they cook together when C. comes to visit.

I ask M. if the food is usually for the family or for the household help as well. 'We always cook for twelve people, including the helpers. We all eat the same food. Eating good food is important, it gives you energy to work well.' M. replies. I find out a little more about her. M. grew up in a village in Chettinad until she was thirteen years old, when her father was transferred to Malaysia, and the family moved there. She came back to Chennai when she was twenty, to get married. Her father was a banker, whose work was linked to the rice trade between India and Burma (Myanmar), at a time when India imported rice from there. 'I remember big terracotta pots filled with salt and turmeric that came to us from Burma.' M. reminisces. Listening to her, all these distant countries connect to each other, and to India, in my head.

Meanwhile, the food's ready. They've cooked two more dishes, one with okra and the other a dal dish from North India, made by G. 'It's nice for G. to have a flavour of home!' says M.

We sit at the dining table, with the food laid out in porcelain plates and bowls. This is rare, for I've usually been served food in stainless steel dishes in most of the kitchens I've visited. I look at the array of dishes: eggplant gravy, banana flower vadai, okra *pachadi* (okra cooked in tamarind sauce), dal and rice. Everything is very tasty and delicately flavoured. 'You must finish up with curd rice, Nao!' says C. I'm already so full and the curd rice (which is what they call rice and yogurt) fills me up even more. I've still not learned to eat in a way that leaves room for curd rice, which is what ends meals in most South Indian homes.

I leave with a satiated feeling. The experience has left me with a feeling of delicious opulence – that, and the faint, complex scent of banana flowers. The memory has stayed with me until this day.

M.'s Vazhaipoo Vadai
Banana Flower Lentil Patties

For 4 people (about 20 pieces)

100 gms toor dal
100 gms channa dal
5 dried red chilli
2 tbsp. fennel seeds
florets from a banana flower
1 onion
lg bunch of coriander leaves
lg sprig of curry leaves
1 tsp. turmeric powder
salt to taste
oil for frying

Soak toor dal and channa dal in water for 2 hours. Soak red chilli and fennel seeds in water in another bowl. Remove the white-and-yellow florets from a banana flower, and remove the bitter inner pistils. Grind the dal and spices together into a coarse batter. Grind in the banana florets into the dal mixture. Make sure the batter is firm, not watery. Add chopped onion, coriander leaves, curry leaves, turmeric and salt to the mixture. Form small balls and flatten each ball out on your palm. Deep fry the vadai in oil.

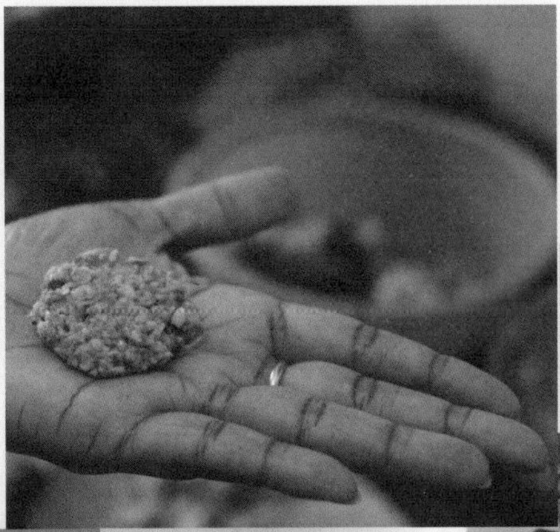

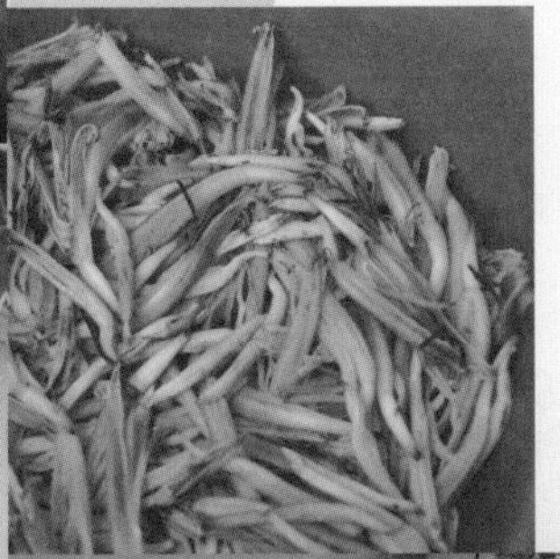

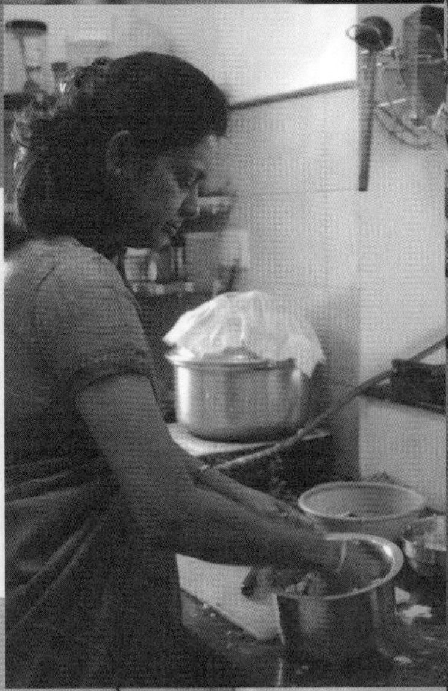

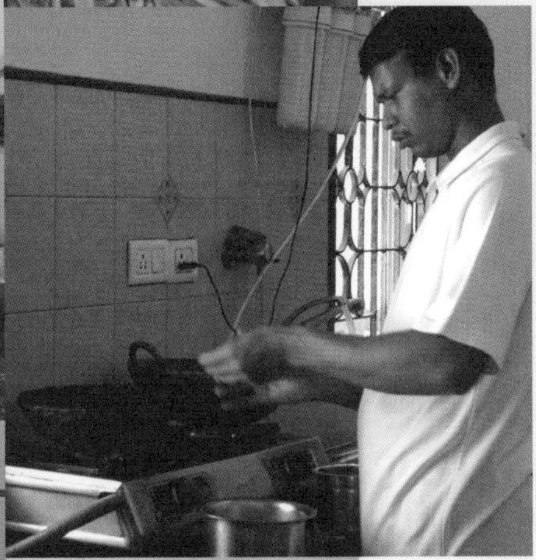

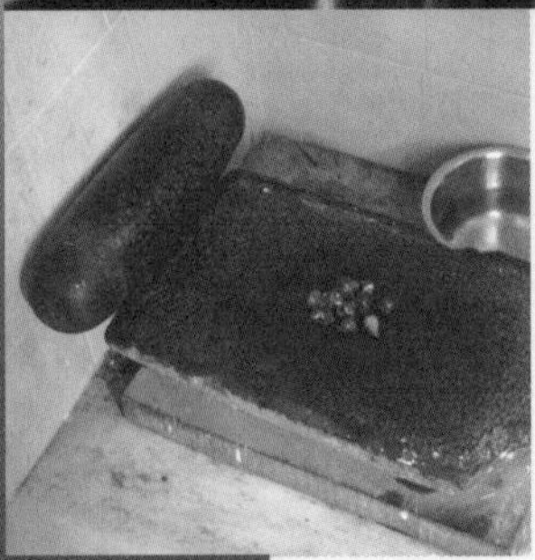

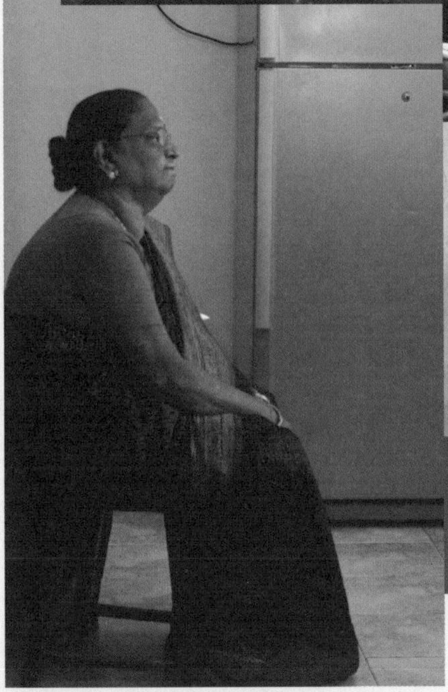

lots of shelves above

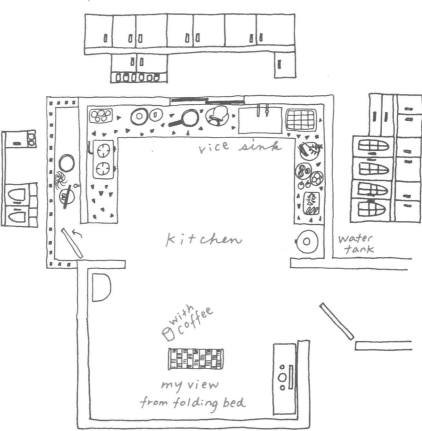

rice sink

kitchen

water tank

with coffee

my view
from folding bed

GIRLS' KITCHEN

lemon $\phi = 45mm$

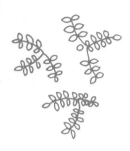

Curry
leaves

V. IS ONE OF MY YOUNGEST FRIENDS HERE IN CHENNAI, introduced to me by mutual friends. She's just started a new job at a local company, and shares a flat with two other young women. I've been asked to come early on my visit to their kitchen, since V. is anxious get to work on time.

So I show up at V.'s apartment at five minutes to eight. I knock at her door and call out her name.

'You here already, Nao?' V. opens the door in her pajamas. She sounds as though she's just woken up. 'Come in, you're an early bird!'

V.'s apartment looks new – it has a living room, kitchen, bathroom and two bedrooms. The living room is bare – it has a shelf and a folded bed. 'Good morning!' says S., who shares the flat with V. The two brush their teeth at the washbasin, standing next to each other.

S. and V. know each other from childhood. They were classmates in high school, in their home city of Madurai. 'We visit Madurai often,' says S. 'At least twice a month.' It's an overnight journey by train or bus. S. is currently studying architecture at a city university, and her final exams begin soon.

'Are you going to be architect?' I ask her.

'No, I want to be in academics.' she replies.

'Would you like some coffee?' asks V., unfolding the bed in the living room for me. I sit there, with a cup of coffee, and watch the girls get busy with cooking. From where I am, I can see the entire kitchen, as if it were a stage. I'm happy to be the sole audience of the play that is to unfold in the kitchen this morning.

There are onions, carrots, curry leaves, coriander and a couple of other vegetables on the kitchen shelf. I can see that they cook daily, and they tell me it's usually once a day. This morning they're going to make their lunch, to carry to work.

'Don't throw away the water after washing the rice!' S. tells V., who's busy rinsing rice. 'I've discovered that rice water is ideal for a footbath. Just try it out for a month, and you'll see how smooth your feet get.'

They're making lemon rice. Lemon rice is good for a lunch box. Its acidic content keeps the rice tasting fresh for a longer time. This reminds me of a popular lunch box menu in Japan: rice balls with plum pickle. There seem to be some common practices that connect India and Japan – maybe because we're both rice eating cultures?

As the rice cooks, V. and S. get busy with the tempering. V. squeezes the juice from a lemon into a cup, and S. sets out the seasoning: mustard seeds, *urad dal*, turmeric, red chillies and curry leaves. Meanwhile, the rice is done, and S. takes charge.

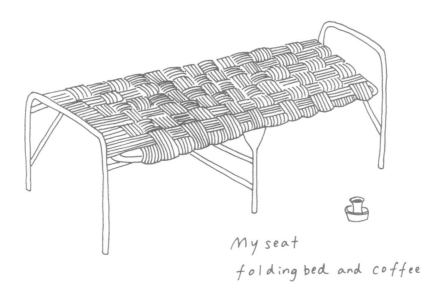

My seat
folding bed and coffee

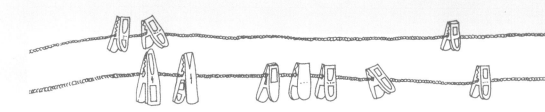

She seems to be more used to cooking, unlike V. who's learning to cook. S. covers the bubbling rice pot with a lid, wraps a towel around the rim to pick it up, and takes it to the kitchen sink. She holds the pot upside down, to drain the extra water out.

S. heats oil in a pan, then adds the seasoning. Once the mustard seeds pop and the other ingredients sizzle, she tips the contents of the pan into the pot of rice. V. adds salt and lemon juice, and gives it a good stir. She takes a small taste of the lemon rice. 'Mmm ... I'm not sure...' she says, and begins to rummage on the shelf. 'When I'm not sure about the taste, I add peanuts. Peanuts make any dish taste good. ' She's finally satisfied, and packs the rice into their lunch boxes – I'm served a portion on a plate.

'How about you?' I ask.

'We don't eat breakfast!' the girls chorus. They get busy with a bucket of water on the balcony, which has an immersion heater in it. Water is being warmed for a bath.

'Good morning!' The two then go into one of the bedrooms to wake up the third girl.

I'm touched to learn that even though there are two rooms, all the three sleep together in one. A sudden blast of Tamil film music comes from the room. Their day has begun.

warm water
for shower

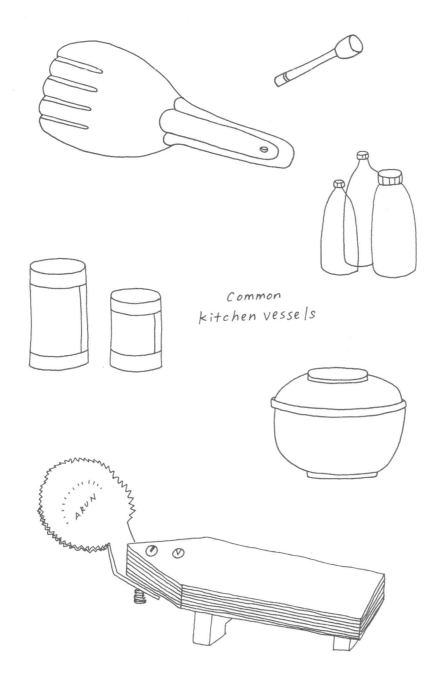

Common
kitchen vessels

S.'s Elimichchai Sadam
Lemon Rice

For 3 people

1 cup rice
1 lemon
1 tsp. mustard seed
1 tsp. urad dal
a few curry leaves
1 tsp. turmeric powder
salt to taste
roasted peanuts (optional)

Rinse the rice and cook in a pot of water, or a pressure cooker. Squeeze the juice out of the lemon. Heat oil in a pan, add mustard seeds, and when they pop, add urad dal and fry until it's golden. Tip in the curry leaves and turmeric. Let the mixture sizzle, then remove from the flame and pour on to the rice. Mix in the lemon juice, and if you like, roasted peanuts.

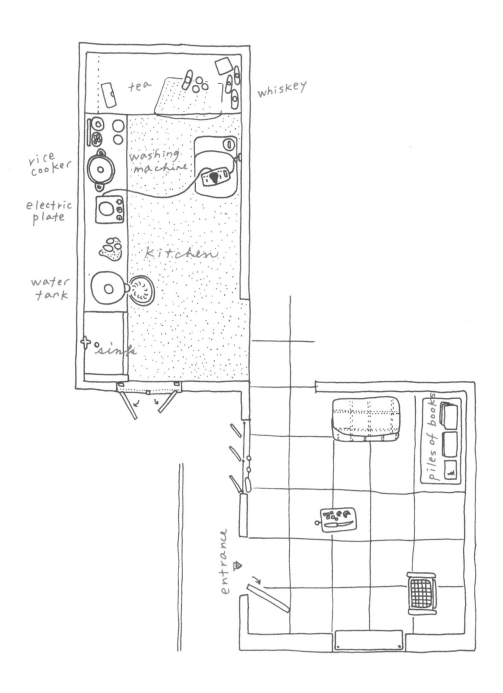

tea

whiskey

rice cooker

washing machine

electric plate

kitchen

water tank

sink

entrance

piles of books

B
A
C
H
E
L
O
R
S'

K
I
T
C
H
E
N

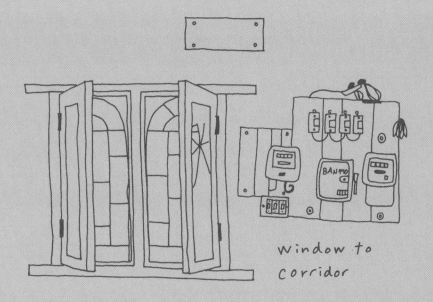

window to
corridor

mineral water
for drinking

I'M ALL SET TO VISIT A BACHELORS' KITCHEN. I've always been curious to discover how single young men cook, and now's my chance to find out. But I must confess that I'm a little uncertain, so I make sure to eat a small lunch before I set out. I admit that I've never done this before visiting any other kitchen, but I'm playing it safe.

M., my new friend, has come to fetch me and we ride on his motorbike to a small apartment in a residential neighbourhood. It's a regular block of flats, painted light yellow. We go up to the second floor, through a winding stairwell. There are two apartments on this floor. I hear the television blaring from the other apartment.

'All these flats are shared by bachelors like us. The rent is high but our landlord's happy to have us, because we don't use much electricity or water and we're good tenants.' M. explains.

His home is tidier than I expected – or maybe there are not too many things in it. I sit on the edge of a folded mattress. 'I'm afraid you'll find this a bit messy...' M. is apologetic.

'No, no! It's much tidier than I expected' I say honestly.

I notice that there's a poster of Marilyn Monroe on the wall. This is
a two-room flat, with a kitchen and bathroom. I'm told that four
people shared the place until recently. 'One of our roommates just
moved out, he got married,' M. tells me, and steps out for a bit. He
returns with a large parcel wrapped in newspaper – it contains rice
which he's just bought from a shop nearby. He also hauls in a new
can of drinking water.

His roommate S. follows, holding a plastic bag with vegetables.
We're introduced, and shake hands. Like the girls I met earlier, these
two young men are childhood friends from the city of Madurai, who
studied together in high school. S. hurries straight into the kitchen,
and pours some water into a pot. He throws in some tomatoes from
his shopping bag, puts his hand into the water and starts to squeeze
them out. I don't think I saw him wash his hands before cooking.
I'm taken aback, but tell myself that it's alright, because if this is for
rasam (tamarind broth), it's going to be boiled anyway.

M. gets out a cutting board, sits down on the floor in the room next to
the kitchen, and starts to chop onions. He chops them very skillfully.
S. joins him and they cut all the vegetables together.

'We were vegetarians until we moved to Chennai,' says M. 'We'd never
eaten meat or eggs.' But in Chennai, all their friends ate meat, so they
started to as well. 'We feel easier eating fish rather than meat. But we
really like eggs, we eat them almost every day!' he adds.

eggs

'How do you like your egg?' I ask. 'Omelet, egg *dosa* (a savoury pancake), egg curry, egg fried rice...?' I know that in South India, egg is a regular dish on the menu, and comes in many forms.

'We like them in all kinds of ways. We'll make an omelet today.' M. unwraps a package from the plastic bag and brings out eggs. I see that they've gone and bought all the ingredients for the lunch they want to cook for me today.

They break the eggs into a bowl, add chopped onions, chilli powder, and salt. The chilli powder makes this an Indian-style omelet. S. puts a pan on the stove, adds a bit of oil and tips the egg mixture into it. They have only one stove – it's an electric hot plate, which is standard equipment in many shared homes. I notice several empty whisky bottles on the shelf. M. points to a blender standing next to them: 'In shared houses like ours people usually don't have a blender. But the way we got this is funny. I once worked with a TV crew that shot a film about a young person in a fishing village. All these kitchen things were used in that film, and I acquired them!'

Meanwhile, lunch is ready: *sambar*, *rasam*, omelet and rice. Very well put together, I think. S. brings the food over from the kitchen to the room where we're sitting, and we all eat together. I take my first bite and find the food very tasty. I tell them so.

'Really? I'm surprised at how well we've cooked today!' says S. and smiles. I get on well with him, as we chat and eat our lunch. As a finale, S. adds some yogurt to the rice leftover in the pot, and finishes the whole thing.

Next time, I'll make sure to visit on an empty stomach.

empty bottle of whiskey
on the shelf.

lunch on newspaper

S.'s Indian Omelet

For 3 people

3 eggs
1 onion
chilli powder to taste
1 tsp. mustard seeds
1 tbsp. oil
salt to taste

Chop the onions. Break the eggs into a bowl. Add the chopped onions, salt and chilli powder. Mix well. Fry mustard seeds in oil in a pan, and then add the egg mixture. Cook until it sets.

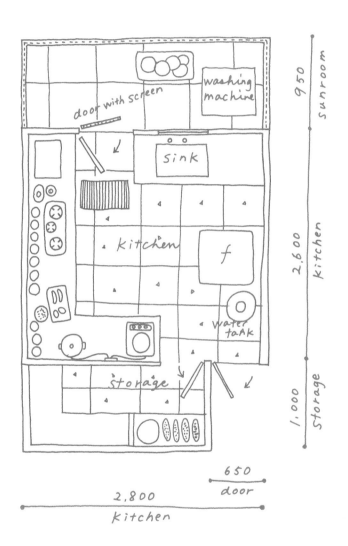

door with screen

washing
machine

sink

kitchen

f

water
tank

storage

950   sunroom

2,600   kitchen

1,000   storage

650
door

2,800
kitchen

COOKING

KITCHEN WITHOUT

guava

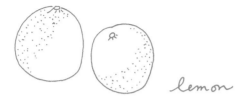

lemon

I'VE ALWAYS BEEN INTRIGUED BY what my colleague, L., eats for lunch. When she unpacks her lunchbox in the office, it's usually filled with something unexpected: carrot sticks, steamed peanuts, or sometimes just an apple. I've always been very curious to see her kitchen, but only manage to visit her on my last day in Chennai, on the morning of my departure to Japan.

It is 6.45 am, and I'm on my way to L.'s house. She lives not far from me, and at this hour, the place is already lively. I go past the local temple and arrive at her apartment, housed in a large building which must be at least a decade old. I greet the guard and go up the stairs to her front door. There's a bag hanging on the handle – it contains a milk packet, which is home delivered every morning.

L. opens the door. 'Come in, Nao!' she greets me. 'Oh, here's the milk! Have you had breakfast?'

I follow her into the kitchen. She puts the milk on to boil, and heats a small pan with water. 'How much sugar do you want in your milk?' she asks. 'Look, this is palm sugar – you dissolve it in warm water and then filter it through, so the dust is taken out. It's a natural product, not treated in any way, which is why you have to clean it.'

I find her style of doing things quite unique.

The doorbell rings. It is her house helper, who's come to wash the dishes. She says something to L. in Tamil. 'She wants me to buy regular dishwashing liquid. We've started using use eco-friendly

detergent, and she thinks it doesn't clean as well as the regular one.'
I understand now why the water in the sink looks slightly cloudy.

L. tells me that two years ago, she decided to buy only organically
grown produce, and since the last two months, has managed to
source good vegetables. 'I'm looking for organic milk,' she adds.
I've been thinking along those lines as well. I realise that even though
we live in different countries, we have similar concerns. Perhaps
both of us are women who belong to a particular generation.

She takes vegetables out of the fridge, ready for chopping: carrot,
cucumber, tomato and mango-ginger.

'Mango ginger is a seasonal thing. I love it. I buy as much as I can
when it's available.' It's a root, and generally used as a condiment.
I love it, too.

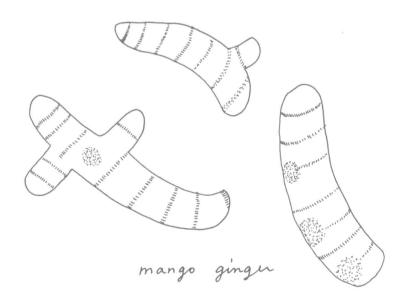

mango ginger

kovaikai

'Nao, come and smell this!' L. exclaims as she chops the mango-ginger. It does have an indescribably fresh scent – a mixture of raw green mango and delicate ginger. I can imagine how it would lift up the salad. L. starts cutting the other vegetables. 'So that's my work in the kitchen – chopping up vegetables. I don't do too much else. But must say I like making salad. I just make sure my salad has some protein in it.' I notice that she's added homemade green *moong* sprouts to the mix. 'Made by my mother,' clarifies L. 'I can't get moong beans to sprout like she can – crisp and long.'

I ask L. if she prefers raw food. 'Not really. I'm simply not interested in cooking. Until I got married, I lived at home, and my mother cooked. She worked at an office, but still managed to cook – not just everyday food, but traditional cuisine with seasonal vegetables, sweets for festivals... and when I got married and moved away, I knew couldn't be like her. But I wanted to make sure that the food we eat is as nutritious as my mother's cooking.'

L. explains that in India, cooking is traditionally viewed as a woman's task, especially a married woman's task. 'People expect a lot from a woman who is married. Everyone wonders about her cooking skills, what she's learnt from her mother... no man would ever be asked these questions.' That's true, I think, and her straightforward way of putting it appeals to me.

L. has come up with a menu plan for the day: warm milk with oats, sweetened with palm sugar, for breakfast – which is what she usually has before leaving for work. Then she's made a salad, to be eaten at 11.00 am. For lunch, she's already cooked rice in the morning, and she's planning to mix it with yogurt, to make curd rice. She also has an apple ready to eat at 3.00 pm.

I understand that she's built a relationship to food that is all her own. I got a sense of it this morning, as I watched her smell a lemon, and hum while cutting vegetables. She doesn't cook much but it's a creative kitchen, and she has her own ways of being happy in it. It's not because of anything her mother taught her, or because someone else expects her to be a certain way.

I ask her about her husband. 'He doesn't know, but he's actually a feminist!' she jokes, straightforward as always. 'Because he does everything else at home, I'm in charge of the kitchen.' she adds.

Humming cheerfully, she packs two lunch boxes, for herself and her husband. We spend some time companionably, reading the newspaper. L. then takes a shower, gets dressed and ready to go to work. This morning, she's wearing a beautiful white scarf.

It's 8.45 when we leave, and I notice that her kitchen is filled with morning light from the veranda. It's very quiet in there, and L.'s husband is glancing through the newspaper. A peaceful morning sight, I think, and feel a sudden sense of empathy for the way they have created something very special together.

It seemed to be a fitting end to my travels.

L.'s Sprout Salad

For 2 people

1 cup of green moong sprouts
3 small cucumbers
2 small carrots
2 tomatoes
1 fresh green pepper
handful of mango ginger
1/2 lemon
salt to taste

Chop all the vegetables, mix with the sprouts,
and add lemon juice and salt to taste.

THE SECRET OF SOUTH INDIAN KITCHENS

How do I sum up my culinary experiences? Maybe with something practical, something which is very typical of this part of the world. If there's one thing that's readily available in almost all South Indian kitchens, it would be the rice and lentil batter which is used to make a range of dishes: *idli, dosa, kuzhi paniyaram...* whenever I arrived at a kitchen, batter was always ready and waiting.

I was told that it takes time to ferment, so the batter is ground the night before. It contains no yeast or any other leavening agent which helps fermentation – the batter rises overnight entirely due to the natural bacteria in the mixture. It's apparently an ancient way of fermenting, known for hundreds of years. These days, of course, not many people use the traditional grinding stone – most kitchens I visited had a modern electric version of it. Two heavy cylindrical stones rotate

rice + lentils
always ready for
making batter

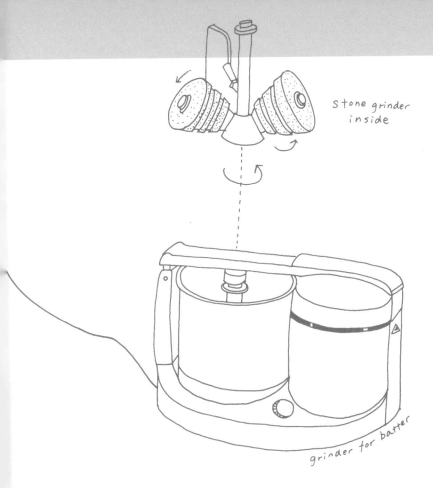

stone grinder inside

grinder for batter

against each other and crush the rice and lentils into a paste.
So air is incorporated into the batter during the process. I learnt that
this makes a big difference to the way the batter rises, in comparison
to grinding it in a blender, which cuts the mixture with a blade, rather
than crushing it. This batter appears to be at the heart of South Indian
food, since everyone I met had their own philosophy about it.

One day, I asked Aunty S. to spend some time with me, to show me
the entire process involved in making it. She said that some people
use differing proportions of rice and lentils to make varying batters
for idlis and dosas, but she herself had a standard recipe, which she
would thin down to make different dishes. Since Aunty S. was the
woman who opened the first door to South Indian kitchens for me,
it seems appropriate that I end with her letting me into its secret.

Aunty S.'s Maavu
Rice and Lentil Batter

3 cups boiled rice (can be substituted with raw rice)
1 cup urad dal
2 tbsp. puffed rice (optional)
1 tbsp. fenugreek seeds

Soak the rice and fenugreek in water for at least three hours. Soak urad dal and puffed rice separately. Drain the water from the bowl with *urad dal*. Grind the dal (you can use a blender if you don't have a stone grinder), using just enough water to make a silky paste. Pour into a large pot. Grind the rice separately to a smooth consistency, it shouldn't be too watery. Add it to the dal, stir, and cover with a lid. In a warm climate, nothing more is needed than to let it sit overnight. It will ferment and rise up to almost double. Stir it thoroughly the next day, and put it in the fridge, it will stay fresh for almost a week. When you want to make idli or dosa, take out the required quantity of dough, and add salt to taste. Thin down the batter to make dosas.

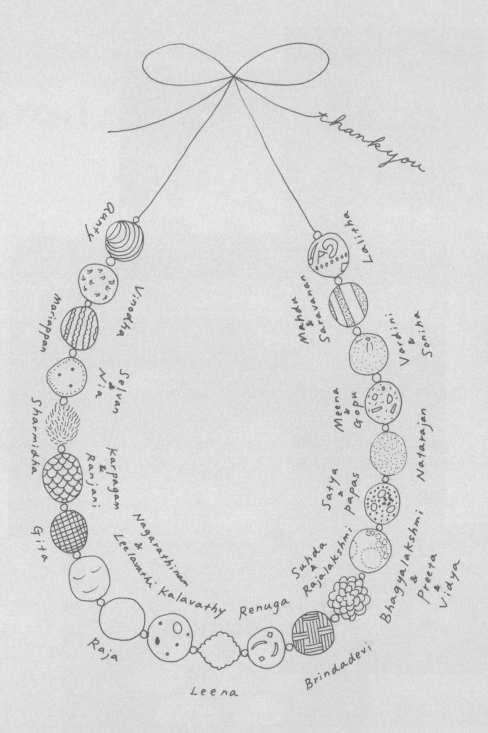

thankyou

In fond memory of Meena

Travels Through South Indian Kitchens
Copyright 2017, Tara Books Pvt. Ltd.
For the text & illustration: Nao Saito

Design: Nia Thandapani
Cover design: Ragini Siruguri
Photographs: Nao Saito, Ragini Siruguri

For this edition:
Tara Books Private Limited, India, www.tarabooks.com
& Tara Books Ltd., UK, www.tarabooks.com/UK

Production: C. Arumugam

Printed in India by Canara Traders and Printers

ISBN: 978-93-83145-59-1

The recipes have been written in keeping with the way in
which Indian cooks describe ingredients and processes in
approximation, rather than through exact measurements and
time taken. Also, to keep it simple, ingredients - like lentils -
have been identified by their commonly used Indian names
rather than through Tamil or other South Indian ones (for
example 'dal' instead of 'paruppu').

Thanks to:

Anveshi, Research Centre for Women's Studies, Hyderabad for permission to
excerpt from 'Beef, Our Life' (Anveshi Broadsheet on Contemporary Politics,
Volume 1, No. 4, *Food Politics and Hegemony*)

and

The Itabashi Museum, Tokyo, for enabling the making of this book.